FROM PRINCIPLE TO PRACTICE

Evidence-Informed Leadership

Edited by the
Chartered College of Teaching

FROM PRINCIPLE TO PRACTICE

Evidence-Informed Leadership

Together we unlock every learner's unique potential

At Hachette Learning (formerly Hodder Education), there's one thing we're certain about. No two students learn the same way. That's why our approach to teaching begins by recognising the needs of individuals first.

Our mission is to allow every learner to fulfil their unique potential by empowering those who teach them. From our expert teaching and learning resources to our digital educational tools that make learning easier and more accessible for all, we provide solutions designed to maximise the impact of learning for every teacher, parent and student.

Aligned to our parent company, Hachette Livre, founded in 1826, we pride ourselves on being a learning solutions provider with a global footprint.

www.hachettelearning.com

Every effort has been made to trace all copyright holders, but if any have been inadvertently overlooked, the Publishers will be pleased to make the necessary arrangements at the first opportunity.

Although every effort has been made to ensure that website addresses are correct at time of going to press, Hachette Learning cannot be held responsible for the content of any website mentioned in this book. It is sometimes possible to find a relocated web page by typing in the address of the home page for a website in the URL window of your browser.

Hachette UK's policy is to use papers that are natural, renewable and recyclable products and made from wood grown in well-managed forests and other controlled sources. The logging and manufacturing processes are expected to conform to the environmental regulations of the country of origin.

To order, please visit www.HachetteLearning.com or contact Customer Service at education@hachette.co.uk / +44 (0)1235 827827.

ISBN: 978 1 0360 0820 8

© Chartered College of Teaching 2025

First published in 2025 by
Hachette Learning, (a trading division of Hodder & Stoughton Limited),
An Hachette UK Company
Carmelite House
50 Victoria Embankment
London EC4Y 0DZ
www.HachetteLearning.com

The authorised representative in the EEA is Hachette Ireland, 8 Castlecourt Centre, Dublin 15, D15 XTP3, Ireland (email: info@hbgi.ie)

Impression   10 9 8 7 6 5 4 3 2 1
Year   2029 2028 2027 2026 2025

All rights reserved. Apart from any use permitted under UK copyright law, no part of this publication may be reproduced or transmitted in any form or by any means, electronic or mechanical, including photocopying and recording, or held within any information storage and retrieval system, without permission in writing from the publisher or under licence from the Copyright Licensing Agency Limited. Further details of such licences (for reprographic reproduction) may be obtained from the Copyright Licensing Agency Limited, www.cla.co.uk

A catalogue record for this title is available from the British Library

Illustrations by DC Graphic Design Limited, Hextable, Kent.
Typeset in the UK
Printed and bound by CPI Group (UK) Ltd, Croydon, CR0 4YY

CONTENTS

Foreword 7
Dame Alison Peacock, CEO, Chartered College of Teaching, UK

Introducing the professional principles 9
Katy Chedzey, Associate Director, Professional Learning and Accreditation, Chartered College of Teaching, UK

Section 1. Professional knowledge

Chapter 1. Teaching and learning, assessment and curriculum:
The pursuit of purpose 18
Chris Larvin, Head of Evaluation and Impact, Teach First, UK

Chapter 2. Supporting evidence-informed pedagogy 24
Stuart Kime, Director of Education, Evidence Based Education, UK

Chapter 3. Leading curriculum 34
Grace Healy, IOE – Faculty of Education and Society, University College London, UK; Department of Education, University of Oxford, UK; David Ross Education Trust, UK

Chapter 4. Purposeful assessment 45
Corinne Settle, Senior Educational Lead for Embedding Formative Assessment, The Schools, Students and Teachers Network (SSAT), UK

Leadership insight: Building a shared understanding of assessment with parents and students 53
Claire Badger, Assistant Head, Teaching and Learning, Godolphin and Latymer School, UK

Chapter 5. Prioritising teacher growth and development 58
Haili Hughes, Director of Education, IRIS Connect, UK; Principal Lecturer, University of Sunderland, UK

Chapter 6. Evidence and context 68
Jess Mahdavi-Gladwell, Deputy Head, Robson House, UK

Leadership insight: Context-responsive leadership 74
Narinder Gill, School Improvement Director, Elevate Multi Academy Trust, UK; Former Headteacher, Hunslet Moor Primary School, UK

Section 2 – Part 1. Professional practice: Leading school development

Chapter 7. Establishing your vision 82
Lekha Sharma, School Improvement Lead – Curriculum and Assessment, Avanti Schools Trust, UK

Chapter 8. Evidence-informed school development 89
Kathryn Morgan, Senior Capacity Improvement Advisor, Teaching School Hubs Council, UK

Chapter 9. Strategic evaluation for school leadership 100
Owen Carter, Co-Founder and Director, ImpactEd Group, UK

Leadership insight: Multi-layered evaluation 108
Angela Schofield, School Improvement and Oracy Advisor, UK

Section 2 – Part 2. Professional practice: Leading a professional culture

Chapter 10. Case study: Creating an inclusive culture 114
Sonia Thompson, Headteacher, St Matthew's CE Primary School, UK

Chapter 11. Developing teacher expertise 121
Sarah Cottinghatt, Head of Learning Design, IRIS Connect, UK

Chapter 12. Taking it forward: Supporting systems 130
Katy Chedzey, Associate Director, Professional Learning and Accreditation, Chartered College of Teaching, UK

Leadership insight: Evaluating a school behaviour system 131
Sam Vickers, CEO, Batley Multi Academy Trust, UK

Appendix: Framework for ethical leadership in education 139

FOREWORD

Dame Alison Peacock, CEO, *Chartered College of Teaching*, UK

I am pleased to provide a few words of congratulations at the beginning of this book. Congratulations to you, the reader, for taking the time to begin wondering about what the research evidence tells us about leadership and how these lessons might be practised in schools of all types. The Chartered College of Teaching aims to build a system-wide community of professional learning. As part of this work, it is vital that we support school leaders to critically examine and develop leadership practice. Our mission is to empower a knowledgeable and respected teaching profession through membership and accreditation. We believe that respect for our profession comes from a combination of factors, including the capacity to take wise leadership decisions based on more than intuition, drawing on a foundation of agency and self-efficacy gained from building a repertoire of leadership skills.

In this book, you will read about the importance of establishing trust among staff teams and wider communities, of the necessity of curriculum alignment, and of building a supportive professional learning culture. Staff effectiveness and retention are achieved through a culture of professional growth, with tailored opportunities for each individual. Building a truly welcoming and supportive culture also attracts diversity and celebrates difference. At the present time, representation of people from global majority backgrounds in school leadership teams is poor. We ask that you, as a leader, expend energy seeking to find and lift up colleagues who may have been unfairly overlooked for opportunities and promotions. An ethnically diverse profession that mirrors the students we teach promises to be a meaningful and joyful one.

You will be aware that to be a school leader is to take on a role packed with challenge. Through engagement with our *Professional Framework* (Chartered College of Teaching, 2024), you will gain a clarity of vision about how best to properly understand and evaluate the impact of the actions you take. Planning with impact in mind is a central tenet of successful leadership and is deeply connected with achievement of overall purpose.

Within these pages, we will take you through ways of enacting the principles that underpin our *Professional Framework* (2024). Each chapter aims to deepen understanding of professional knowledge, practice and behaviours and has been written by colleagues with a range of practical and academic experience. The virtues that underpin our framework are trust, wisdom, kindness, justice, service, courage and optimism. These virtues were identified within the Framework for Ethical Leadership in Education, developed in 2017 by a commission led by Carolyn Roberts and convened by the Association of School and College Leaders (ASCL, 2019). Reported on in 2019, the framework has been reproduced as an appendix at the end of this book, and is intended to guide colleagues at all stages of their leadership journey. The Framework for Ethical Leadership in education, combined with our own *Professional Framework* (2024), sets a high ethical standard for the profession. They provide foundations that the Chartered College of Teaching hopes to build upon as we move towards establishing greater authority, status, esteem and prestige for the teaching profession.

References

ASCL (2019) *Navigating the educational moral maze: The final report of the Ethical Leadership Commission*. Available at: www.ascl.org.uk/ASCL/media/ASCL/Our%20view/Campaigns/Navigating-the-educational-moral-maze.pdf (accessed 27 March 2025).

Chartered College of Teaching (2024) *Professional Framework*. Available at: https://chartered.college/professional-framework (accessed 29 November 2024).

Introducing the professional principles

Katy Chedzey, Associate Director, Professional Learning and Accreditation, Chartered College of Teaching, UK

Through contributed chapters, this book will explore 14 professional principles that aim to articulate the knowledge, skills and behaviours of the most effective school and trust leaders. These professional principles define the standard that leaders are required to meet to be awarded Chartered Status, and form part of the Chartered College of Teaching's *Professional Framework* (2024), which is designed to support career progression and help to drive meaningful professional learning for teachers and leaders at all stages of their careers.

When developing these principles, we sought input from teachers and school leaders across the country, and delved into the evidence base around effective school leadership. We were keen to avoid reinforcing ideas that effective leaders might have particular character traits, such as being 'inspirational' or 'courageous', as these can be somewhat woolly, particularly in terms of how we might conceptualise, measure or – most importantly – develop such traits. Instead, we sought to understand the specific leadership knowledge and practices that might contribute to achieving strong positive outcomes for children and young people. Of course, this is a challenge, as measures of outcomes typically focus on academic achievements and ignore many of the wider outcomes that leaders strive for in their schools (Day et al., 2020). Furthermore, leaders tend to have a more indirect impact on student outcomes (Leithwood et al., 2019) and therefore claims about leaders' impact may often be based on correlation rather than causation (Coe, 2022).

Nonetheless, there is a strong consensus that effective teaching contributes significantly to improving student outcomes, and so for school leaders, perhaps the greatest opportunity for impact may be to positively influence teaching and learning practices within the school (Leithwood et al., 2019; Robinson, 2007).

As Viviane Robinson explains:

> *'Leadership theory, research and practice needs to be more closely linked to research on effective teaching, so that there is greater focus on what leaders need to know and do to support teachers in using the pedagogical practices that raise achievement and reduce disparity.'* (Robinson, 2007, p. 12)

Drawing on the professional principles, this book attempts to answer the question of what leaders need to know and do to facilitate high-quality teaching and learning in their schools. These principles are grouped into three distinct yet overlapping strands, which form the structure of this book: professional knowledge, professional practice and professional behaviours.

Professional knowledge

These principles cover the broad areas that we believe highly effective leaders should *know* and *understand* deeply, incorporating:

- knowledge of teaching and learning, curriculum and assessment practice
- an understanding of their school, as well as the wider educational context
- an understanding of the characteristics of effective professional development.

Professional practice

These principles aim to capture what highly effective leaders might *do* in their schools to really make a positive difference. These principles fit into two categories:

1. Leading school development, demonstrating:

- a clear vision focused on achieving ambitious (and equitable) outcomes
- critical evaluation and reflection to inform strategic choices
- an evidence-informed approach to school development activity.

2. Leading a professional culture, characterised by:
- a focus on developing teacher expertise and a culture of high-quality teaching
- a culture of learning, belonging and high expectations
- effective systems and processes that support teaching and learning.

Professional behaviours

These principles intend to recognise some of the internal behaviours that might play a facilitating role in leaders' development. Internal behaviours inform actions and, in turn, the impact that leaders have in their settings.

There are five professional behaviours that we have identified as being particularly important, each of which are worthy of further discussion here.

1. Critically evaluates and reflects on their own practice

One of the behaviours that we regularly observe in leaders who attain Chartered Status is that they take time to think deeply about their own practice. They are careful not to jump to conclusions; rather they use evidence drawn from both education research and their own lived experience, using this as the basis for reflecting on their own effectiveness and evaluating the wider impact of what they do. Such leaders have an acute awareness of the strengths and limitations to their thinking, understanding and practice. They are aware of their biases, are cognisant of what they know (and do not yet know), draw out connections and implications, and actively seek out alternative perspectives and new ideas to challenge and extend their thinking.

2. Is committed to engaging in relevant, career-long professional learning

The *Standard for teachers' professional development* (DfE, 2016) emphasises that professional development must be prioritised by school leadership – an idea that is explored and revisited at multiple points throughout this book. As a school leader, there is a responsibility to promote the value of professional learning, to encourage colleagues to engage in relevant, career-long professional learning and development, and to facilitate this where possible. However, it is important that leaders also prioritise their *own* professional learning. Leaders who do this well are astute at identifying their own developmental needs, and proactively seek out formal and informal professional learning opportunities, ensuring that they maintain up-to-date knowledge and continue to develop within their roles.

3. Exhibits and encourages collegiality by supporting and learning from others

An expectation for all Chartered Teachers, whether school leaders or practising classroom teachers, is that they recognise the value of collegiality and actively seek to build and promote this in their own schools and more widely within the profession. A key feature of collegiality is that it is reciprocal, often characterised by a culture of collaborative inquiry whereby individuals are open to sharing practice, sharing knowledge and expertise, and learning from one another. We may see this collegiality enacted in a multitude of ways – for example, the way in which a teacher or leader provides feedback to a colleague through a collaborative and supportive professional discussion; or the way in which a teacher or leader actively engages with or contributes to a professional network to disseminate and/or develop new knowledge, ultimately helping to build a collective knowledge base for the profession.

4. Models high standards of professionalism

In 2024, the Chartered College of Teaching published a working paper titled *Revisiting the notion of teacher professionalism*, which strives to 'redefine what we mean by teacher professionalism and advocate for a more aspirational vision for our profession' (Müller and Cook, 2024, p. 4). The report highlights the complexity of defining 'professionalism' as a concept, but posits a working definition of professionalism as encompassing three domains: the cognitive domain (i.e. a shared body of knowledge and the integration of theory, evidence and skill drawn from experience), the ethical domain (recognising a collective commitment to the greater good, but the need to 'strike a careful balance between teachers' commitments to their students and their own mental health and wellbeing' (p. 14)) and the legal and social domains (the professional standards and regulation of teaching as a profession).

Each domain overlaps, with professional development (PD) and professional identity sitting at the heart of the Venn diagram that can be seen in **Figure 1**.

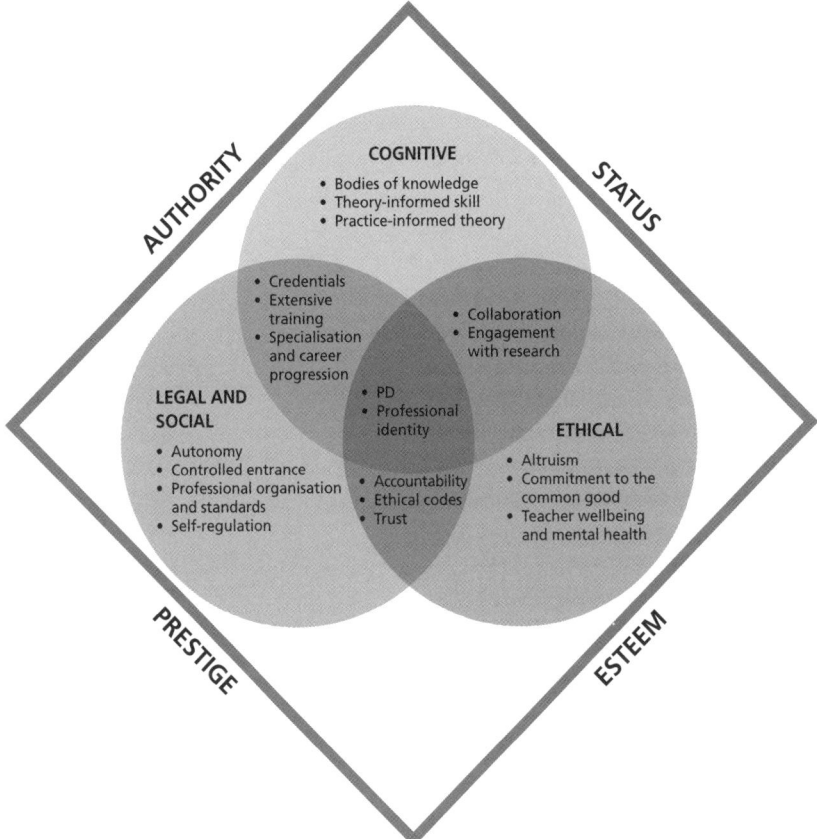

Figure 1: Working definition of professionalism (Müller and Cook, 2024, adapted from Mezza, 2022).

Authority, prestige, esteem and status sit outside the Venn diagram, as these are presented as outcomes that may develop from those mechanisms captured within.

This definition challenges us to reframe our view of professionalism beyond what we might typically understand it to mean, and to reflect on its complexity and implications for our individual and collective identities.

5. Engages critically with research and evidence

The final professional behaviour reflects the need for *critical* engagement with research and evidence. This requires what we might call 'research literacy' – having the confidence to evaluate the quality of education research, to recognise the strengths and limitations of research methodologies, and to interpret research findings in order to translate key ideas into a particular school context, for example.

Beyond research evidence, it's also important to recognise the role that wider evidence may play in terms of implementing evidence-informed approaches and supporting leadership decision-making. The term 'evidence' may include a range of other qualitative and quantitative data that could be gathered formally or informally, and which can help to build a picture of the effectiveness of an approach, in terms of understanding either what is happening *now* in a school or what *might work* in future. Alongside this, there must be space for individuals to exert their own professional judgement and to recognise that teachers and leaders are well positioned to integrate learning from research alongside learning from their own professional experiences within classrooms and schools (Scutt, 2018).

These five professional behaviours transcend the other professional principles; they are overarching and, as such, will not each have their own dedicated chapter but will be exemplified in the voices of those who have contributed to this book as they explore each principle in turn and draw out the key implications – from principle to practice.

References

Chartered College of Teaching (2024) *Professional Framework*. Available at: https://chartered.college/professional-framework (accessed 29 November 2024).

Coe R (2022) Methodological challenges in school leadership research. *School environment and leadership: Evidence review*. Evidence Based Education. Available at: https://evidencebased.education/school-environment-and-leadership-evidence-review (accessed 29 November 2024).

Day C, Sammons P and Gorgen K (2020) *Successful school leadership*. Education Development Trust. Available at: https://edt.org/research-and-insights/successful-school-leadership-2020-publication (accessed 29 November 2024).

Department for Education (DfE) (2016) *Standard for teachers' professional development.* Available at: https://gov.uk/government/publications/standard-for-teachers-professional-development (accessed 29 November 2024).

Leithwood K, Harris A and Hopkins D (2019) Seven strong claims about successful school leadership revisited. *School Leadership & Management* 40(1): 1–18.

Mezza A (2022) Reinforcing and innovating teacher professionalism: Learning from other professions. OECD *Education Working Papers* No. 276. Organisation for Economic Co-operation and Development. Available at: https://oecd.org/en/publications/reinforcing-and-innovating-teacher-professionalism_117a675c-en.html (accessed 17 December 2024).

Müller L-M and Cook V (2024) *Revisiting the notion of teacher professionalism: A working paper.* Chartered College of Teaching. Available at: https://chartered.college/professionalism-report (accessed 29 November 2024).

Robinson V (2007) *The impact of leadership on student outcomes: Making sense of the evidence.* Australian Council for Educational Research. Available at: https://research.acer.edu.au/cgi/viewcontent.cgi?article=1006&context=research_conference_2007 (accessed 4 December 2024).

Scutt C (2018) Is engaging with and in research a worthwhile investment for teachers? In: Carden C (ed) *Primary Teaching: Learning and Teaching in Primary Schools Today.* London: SAGE, pp. 595–610.

SECTION 1
Professional knowledge

PROFESSIONAL PRINCIPLE 1

Leaders demonstrate comprehensive knowledge of teaching and learning, curriculum and assessment

CHAPTER 1

Teaching and learning, assessment and curriculum: The pursuit of purpose

Chris Larvin, *Head of Evaluation and Impact, Teach First, UK*

Teaching and learning, curriculum and assessment collectively define the purpose and impact of education. Each of these topics will be discussed in turn within the subsequent chapters of this book. By way of an introduction, this chapter explores the interconnectedness of these domains and aims to prompt reflection on how they can best serve the needs of our school communities.

What is the purpose of education? Is it primarily about certifying students and signalling their readiness for next steps, or is it about fostering the holistic development of the whole child and nurturing their cognitive abilities, in unison with their social, emotional and physical development? Consider Gert Biesta's (2009) provocation: Are we measuring what we truly value, or are we simply valuing what we can measure? In many schools, attainment and accountability measures dominate, risking the neglect of critical aspects of children's development and inclusion – both pressing issues amid widening poverty and health disparities (Academy of Medical Sciences, 2024). Evidence suggests that prioritising a holistic approach – focusing on the whole child – not only fosters resilience and lifelong learning but also enhances attainment and can reduce educational inequalities (Griffiths et al., 2024). Leaders who align the domains of teaching and learning, curriculum and assessment with a broader purpose of education are better equipped to prepare students for life beyond the school gates.

Creating coherence

What is the role of curriculum if not a list of testable knowledge and skills? Originating from the Latin *currere*, meaning 'to run a course' (Pinar, 2019), curriculum serves as a blueprint for students' development. Leaders are responsible for a carefully sequenced framework to establish both immediate and long-term goals for students, wherein each activity and piece of knowledge contributes to a cohesive whole (Myatt, 2018).

Understanding and supporting curriculum coherence can be challenging. The planned (or intended) curriculum must be well specified and clearly understood to avoid ambiguity. The concept of 'powerful knowledge' (Young and Muller, 2013) can imbue subject matter with intrinsic value and explanatory power, engaging students with complex ideas and building deeper understanding. To achieve this, the planned curriculum should be intentionally sequenced with both inter- and intra-disciplinary development. For example, over a sequence of maths lessons, students attain mastery in the use of coordinates, which grows in complexity, reflecting vertical coherence – building on previous knowledge. Applying grid references in a later geography lesson can reinforce very similar concepts, reflecting horizontal coherence – aligning knowledge across different subjects. The implementation of the planned curriculum reveals the enacted (or taught) curriculum. This represents the extent to which the planned curriculum is taught consistently and with fidelity across the different classrooms within your school. Being able to understand what students have learned – the experienced (learned) curriculum – requires leaders to understand whether or not students are able to build on prior knowledge and deepen meaningful connections to their learning.

As leaders, how can we ensure that the planned curriculum is clearly articulated and understood, such that it can be consistently enacted across classrooms? What approaches and resources can be utilised to identify and close gaps between the planned, enacted and experienced curriculum?

Aligning assessment

Perfect alignment between the planned and experienced curriculum and assessment might seem unnecessary. However, assessment is not just a tool for measuring learning; it also shapes what is taught and how it is taught (Stobart, 2008). Assessment has a key role to play in supporting teaching and learning by generating actionable feedback to both teachers and students, as well as translating abstract curriculum objectives into measurable achievement. However, tensions often arise when the purpose of education intersects with the functions of assessment. Formative assessment provides real-time insights to adjust teaching and is critical to fostering students' development. But overemphasis on summative assessment can narrow the curriculum and focus excessively on measurable outcomes, potentially at the expense of deeper learning and students' ability to self-regulate their learning (Black and Wiliam, 2009). Effective leaders are able to ensure balance of these functions to make sure that assessment does not become a measure of progress against the planned curriculum, but actively aids the learning in support of the curriculum's broader purpose. How can you ensure that it is the planned curriculum that is driving assessment design and use, rather than working in the other direction? Leaders require assessment literacy to ensure that assessments genuinely reflect and support students' development (Richardson, 2022), as well as to resist the undue influence of high-stakes examinations to 'teach to the test' or adopt assessment approaches that arguably conflict with the purpose of education.

A review of students' responses might quickly highlight that assessment is imperfect, given the unpredictability of classrooms and students' cognition. But it remains our best tool for gauging learning, readiness to progress and areas for further attention. Yet to truly serve its purpose, assessment must connect immediate insights to overarching educational goals, ensuring that every student benefits from a curriculum that supports both understanding and long-term growth. Thus, assessment becomes not just a measure of success but also a catalyst for improving teaching and learning.

Leading to realise purpose

Teaching brings the curriculum to life, transforming curriculum intentions into meaningful learning experiences for students. Yet even the most skilled teachers may struggle to support students' development without adequate support or a school culture that enables professional autonomy. Leaders play a significant role in supporting teachers to navigate the complexity of translating the planned curriculum into what is enacted and taught, by prompting reflection of their approaches and providing intelligent accountability to address curriculum misalignment. By providing resources and facilitating training in assessment literacy and evidence-based teaching practices, teachers are better able to enact the planned curriculum and meaningfully integrate assessment. Curriculum alignment does not just ensure that learning reflects the intent of the curriculum; it also helps us to meet the diverse needs of all students, including those with special educational needs and disabilities (SEND). Inclusion should extend beyond teaching, with representation important in all domains. Leaders can risk reinforcing a narrow interpretation of valuable knowledge, sidelining students' diverse perspectives and disconnecting the curriculum from their lived experiences, with poor assessment practices entrenching these inequalities. Research has found that the integration of diverse viewpoints, whether highlighting contributions of women in STEM (science, technology, engineering and mathematics) or incorporating an ethnically diverse array of authors in humanities subjects, enhances relevance and impact for all students (Schneider and Preckel, 2017).

Leading curriculum, assessment and teaching requires more than technical expertise; it demands a clear sense of purpose. Leaders must constantly evaluate and refine their practices, ensuring that they remain aligned with the values of their school and the needs of their students. Recognising and ensuring consistency of purpose across the three domains requires vigilance to the unintended consequences of focusing too narrowly on any one area. While data-driven decision-making is a crucial aspect of school leadership, overemphasis on summative assessment risks reducing education to measurable outcomes alone, potentially constraining the curriculum, limiting teachers' strategies and autonomy, and neglecting students' holistic development (Priestley et al., 2015). Similarly, while improving the quality of teaching is a powerful lever for enhancing student outcomes (Coe et al., 2014), without a robust curriculum to underpin teaching, and teachers equipped with the necessary assessment literacy, such improvements may be limited or unsustainable.

By anchoring leadership to a clear sense of purpose, leaders can ensure that their schools are places of meaningful learning, where every student can thrive academically, socially and emotionally. So, how can we ensure that we are leading these domains with purpose, rather than allowing systems and policies to lead us? In addressing this question with intentionality and care, leaders can equip students with the knowledge, skills and resilience required to engage thoughtfully with the complexities of the rapidly evolving world that lies beyond the school gates.

References

Academy of Medical Sciences (2024) *Prioritising early childhood to promote the nation's health, wellbeing and prosperity*. Available at: https://acmedsci.ac.uk/file-download/16927511 (accessed 1 September 2024).

Biesta G (2009) Good education in an age of measurement: On the need to reconnect with the question of purpose in education. *Educational Assessment, Evaluation and Accountability* 21(1): 33–46.

Black P and Wiliam D (2009) Developing the theory of formative assessment. *Educational Assessment, Evaluation and Accountability* 21(1): 5–31.

Coe R, Aloisi C, Higgins S et al. (2014) *What makes great teaching? Review of the underpinning research*. The Sutton Trust. Available at: https://suttontrust.com/wp-content/uploads/2014/10/What-Makes-Great-Teaching-REPORT.pdf (accessed 1 September 2024).

Griffiths J, Greany T, Penacchia J et al. (2024) Belonging schools: How do relatively more inclusive secondary schools approach and practice inclusion? *Impact* 20: 28–31.

Myatt M (2018) *The Curriculum: Gallimaufry to Coherence*. Woodbridge: John Catt Educational.

Pinar WF (2019) *What is Curriculum Theory?* 2nd ed. New York: Routledge.

Priestley M, Biesta G and Robinson S (2015) *Teacher Agency: An Ecological Approach*. London: Bloomsbury.

Richardson M (2022) *Rebuilding Public Confidence in Educational Assessment*. London: UCL Press.

Schneider M and Preckel F (2017) Variables associated with achievement in higher education: A systematic review of meta-analyses. *Psychological Bulletin* 143(6): 565–600.

Stobart G (2008) *Testing Times: The Uses and Abuses of Assessment*. Abingdon: Routledge.

Young M and Muller J (2013) On the powers of powerful knowledge. *Review of Education* 1(3): 229–250.

CHAPTER 2

Supporting evidence-informed pedagogy

Stuart Kime, *Director of Education, Evidence Based Education, UK*

> **This chapter will consider:**
> - the key evidence-informed pedagogical approaches that leaders should be aware of
> - the implications for school leadership
> - any cautions that leaders should apply when it comes to evidence-informed practice.

For most leaders, building their knowledge and understanding of the things that highly effective teachers 'know, do and care about' (Hattie, 2003, p. 2) should be a priority. But why?

Such knowledge and understanding are the underpinning foundations of adaptive expertise (Lin et al., 2007). Teachers need this knowledge so that they can adapt their practices sensitively and effectively to the needs of their learners. As a leader, you need this knowledge so that you are able to see and remove the barriers that your teachers face in developing, sustaining and deploying their adaptive expertise.

For example, building understanding of key evidence-informed principles can help you to plan and deploy a more responsive and motivating professional development (PD) programme that is informed by both the individual training and development needs identified in a supportive appraisal process, as well as the most robust 'best bet' drawn from the best available research evidence.

Thankfully, these robust 'best bets' have been reviewed and summarised to help you to focus on the things most likely to make an impact on student learning.

What are some of the key evidence-informed pedagogical approaches of which leaders should be aware?

Evidence Based Education's *Great Teaching Toolkit: Evidence Review* (Coe et al., 2020) presents a clear, common language to describe the things that highly effective teachers know, do and believe. The review puts forward four key evidence-informed pedagogical approaches that, as a leader, you should keep in mind when supporting effective teaching in your school or trust:

1. The most effective teachers **understand the content** that they are teaching and how it is learned. In practice, a key characteristic of effective teachers is 'deep and fluent knowledge, and flexible understanding of the content they are teaching and how it is learnt, including its inherent dependencies. They should have an explicit repertoire of well-crafted explanations, examples and tasks for each topic they teach.' (Coe et al., 2020, p. 17)

2. The most effective teachers **create a supportive environment** for learning. That environment – be it a classroom, sports field, science lab or drama studio – is 'characterised by relationships of trust and respect between students and teachers, and among students. It is one in which students are motivated, supported and challenged and have a positive attitude towards their learning.' (Coe et al., 2020, p. 22)

3. Understand the importance of managing the classroom in order to **maximise every opportunity that students have to learn**. Classroom management is a common topic, but rarely is it given an explicit learning focus. However, the evidence is clear that, while different teachers have different styles, values and priorities, the common thread is that effective teachers use the resources and time that they have available for maximum impact on learning (Coe et al., 2020).

4. Finally, the **activation of hard thinking** cuts right to the heart of effective classroom practice. This is about explanations, questions, feedback, practice tasks and sequences of scaffolded (and

unscaffolded) learning tasks that teachers deploy to get learners thinking hard about the material that they want them to learn. It's also probably the trickiest part of the job to learn, mainly because the feedback that teachers get is unreliable and insufficient. Learning is invisible, slow and nonlinear, so it's incredibly hard for teachers to know whether it's even happening (Coe et al., 2020).

There is no substitute for you and your teachers sharing a common understanding of the elements of great teaching, nor is there a substitute for a shared language of pedagogy. Both of these help leaders to build coherent and consistent performance management and appraisal processes. Indeed, without these, professional communication within schools and between colleagues is always going to be unclear, inefficient and at odds with our collective aims to improve outcomes both for learners and for those who teach them.

What are the implications for school leadership?

Before we look at the key evidence-informed pedagogical approaches that leaders should be aware of in more detail, it will be helpful to further think about some of the implications they have for school leadership. Two important overarching principles should be considered.

Principle 1: All the approaches matter, but they will matter in different ways for different teachers

Just as learners have different prior knowledge, understanding and skills, every teacher has different strengths and areas for growth. Teachers of the same subject or phase, who work together every day in the same school, may have very different developmental needs. The challenge for school leadership comes when this fact is acknowledged and the need for tailored, personalised professional development emerges. Yet, if leaders are to help teachers to develop their adaptive expertise, this is a challenge that must be addressed constructively. One size does not fit all for classroom learning; nor does it for professional learning.

Principle 2: Shining a spotlight on one approach can cast others into the shadows

Leadership in schools – as in all organisations – involves a considerable amount of prioritisation. It's about choosing to do some things and choosing not to do others. When, as a leader, you choose to shine a spotlight on one approach – to focus your own and your colleagues' attention and energy on it – this choice comes with the risk of casting the other three into the shadows. It opens up the possibility of diminishing their importance and relevance, as well as their interconnectedness. There is an opportunity cost to such a choice, one that all leaders should hold in mind when making strategic choices.

For example, the increased interest in cognitive psychology and the science of learning has, in recent years, shone a spotlight on important features of the learning process, such as attention and working memory capacity. This is, arguably, a good thing. But in shining such a bright spotlight on cognitive aspects of learning, have we inadvertently cast the affective aspects of learning into the shadows?

Ultimately, time is finite and as a leader you must make choices about where to focus the collective attention of the teaching and leadership community in your school. Arguably, an important role for leaders in schools is to ensure that these four key pedagogical approaches remain in the light at all times, even when the spotlight is turned up on one.

We will now consider some more specific aspects of each of the four key pedagogical approaches mentioned earlier.

1. Understanding the content

Strategic recruitment

Leaders should prioritise recruiting, retaining and developing teachers with strong subject knowledge, as well as a deep understanding of effective pedagogy. Collective teacher expertise has a measurable impact on individual teacher effectiveness, so the recruitment and development of each individual matters for the whole team, not just for the individual. This also has implications for how PD is structured: collaboration, feedback and expertise-sharing should be central, with the purpose of improving all and not just one.

Supportive collaboration

Leaders should focus on fostering trust and collaboration among staff in the work of curriculum development, emphasising the shared responsibility for high-quality teaching materials. On the face of it, ready-made curricula and emerging AI-based tools may make this activity appear redundant, but they lack the vital component of teachers thinking hard together about the content that they will teach. Such thinking is a mainstay of adaptive expertise development.

2. Creating a supportive environment

Safe and inclusive school climate

Teachers can influence their classroom environments, but leaders set the tone for the wider school environment. Therefore, it's helpful to establish and model relationships with colleagues and learners that have warmth, empathy and mutual trust at their core. Such modelling can help to create the social norms of the school and classroom for all who come together in the community of your setting.

Purpose and belonging

Developing strategies to enhance students' sense of belonging and connection to the school community is important for promoting motivation and engagement. To achieve this, leaders should seek to build a sense of belonging by promoting a sense of purpose in learning that goes far beyond the short-term self-interest of 'doing well on tests', but which doesn't fall into the trap of abstract long-termism ('learning this will help you if you become an accountant'). Purpose in learning (for example, learning about water pollution in the local area so that learners can write a letter to the local council calling for action) can be a powerful tool for creating a collective bond that reaches far beyond self-interest.

3. Maximising opportunities to learn

Optimised learning time

More time equals more opportunity. Leaders should, therefore, conduct regular reviews of how teaching time is allocated and used. You should also focus on minimising disruptions to classrooms – for example, unnecessary announcements (e.g. over a tannoy system) or poorly planned timetable changes. Conducting a time audit of the school day to identify inefficiencies (such as lengthy transitions between lessons, excessive time spent on administrative tasks or the sources of interruption to lessons) is one way in which leaders can positively impact the quality of interactions in the classroom.

Positive behaviour management

Training and supporting school staff in 'antecedent' strategies (Kern and Clemens, 2007), designed to help them to anticipate and de-escalate behaviour and dysregulation issues before they disrupt learning, is one way in which leaders can help to maximise the opportunity that every learner has to learn. Equally, developing a consistent, coherent school-wide system to quickly resolve minor disruptions and ensure that learning is minimally affected is another implication of this pedagogical principle.

4. Activating hard thinking

Challenging expectations

Teachers and leaders should set a high bar for all students and staff by communicating clear, ambitious goals. Such goals should, ideally, be FAST goals: frequently discussed, ambitious, specific and transparent – rather than SMART goals: specific, measurable, achievable, relevant and time-bound. SMART goals can focus too much on individual performance (the opposite of what is needed for collective expertise-building in a school) and ignore the critical role of an ongoing discussion of goals throughout the year.

But these high expectations and goals should also operate in an environment of high trust, where everyone feels that it's okay to 'have a go', and to attribute successes and failures to their own actions. One of the most powerful ways in which leaders can create this kind of environment is to model to the community the experience – the highs and the lows – of working to achieve challenging, purposeful goals.

Efficacy and agency

Belief in the power of teaching to make a positive difference to learners' lives can make a huge difference to the motivations of teachers and leaders. It gives a defined purpose and drive to the daily work of schools and colleges. As a leader, you can help teachers to feel more confident, and competent, in their ability to make a difference by providing actionable feedback and access to personalised professional learning (a key to unlocking and developing adaptive expertise). And, just as would be considered the norm for students in schools and colleges, leaders should celebrate professional learning successes, while also encouraging reflective practices for ongoing improvement.

What cautions should leaders apply when it comes to evidence-informed practice?

Justifying decisions in ways that are informed by the best available evidence of likely effects is at the heart of evidence-informed practice for leadership. Understanding the four key approaches and making decisions that promote these should be a core part of your leadership role. But what are the limitations of evidence-informed practice?

Research is from the past; it can't tell leaders what to do

The first limitation is that even the best available research evidence is limited; it's always a snapshot of certain people, certain phenomena and certain contexts, and it's always from the past. It can't tell anyone what to do but it can shed useful light on what happened when someone did something similar to that which you might be planning. Understanding this offers a hugely important caution when considering the adoption of a new programme or initiative in a school.

Take, for example, the research evidence on instructional coaching. While there is some good evidence to support the deployment of instructional coaching, Kraft et al. (2018) found that larger coaching had smaller effects. They also pointed out the difficulty in recruiting effective coaches. Coaching, the researchers warned, shouldn't be viewed as a broad, generalised solution to the problems of PD. Instead, they said: 'It may be that coaching is best utilised as a targeted program with a small corps of expert coaches working with willing participants and committed schools rather than as a district-wide PD program.' (p. 574) And, despite the evidence on coaching, the researchers were unable to say which approaches to coaching were most effective, although there is some evidence that the expertise of the coach is a key driver (Blazar and Kraft, 2015). There is also some evidence that more effective coaches may also be more effective teachers (Blazar et al., 2021; Goldhaber et al., 2020).

Research will present new, uncomfortable challenges

The second limitation is that while there is a good and growing body of evidence to help leaders make strategic and operational decisions, implementation of these in the real-world context of a specific setting presents leaders with new, uncomfortable challenges to their prior knowledge and practices. To understand this more, the concrete example of feedback to teachers is helpful.

Even though most teachers and leaders would acknowledge the power of feedback for students' learning, what they encounter in their own professional learning compares very poorly. Growth in complex activities like teaching depends on good, easily generated feedback. Yet most teachers receive very limited feedback about their performance that is actionable and timely.

Teachers are constantly evaluating how well a lesson is going and looking for signs of confusion or waning interest, but these are often what Rob Coe (2013) has called 'poor proxies' for the feedback that teachers really need. They also receive feedback from lesson observations – either as part of a coaching, mentoring or appraisal process – but the judgements made by observers who do not have specialised training for the role are generally wrong (Coe, 2014), and that inaccuracy has damaging consequences for the feedback that teachers receive.

The evidence points in one direction, but convention, policy and trend may point in another. In these circumstances, the limitation of evidence-informed practice comes less from the evidence itself and more from how leaders understand it and respond to its uncomfortable challenges.

Conclusion

As a leader, you need to know what the research says in relation to the decisions that you intend to make. And because you make decisions that directly and indirectly impact the classroom interactions that are the beating heart of the teaching and learning in your setting, it's critical that you have a deep and full understanding of the evidence-informed pedagogical principles and approaches highlighted in this chapter.

These understandings are made easier with modern frameworks like A Model for Great Teaching presented in the *Great Teaching Toolkit: Evidence Review* (Coe et al., 2020). But they still depend on your thinking hard about them and interpreting them for your specific context. Your own learning matters here. But the time and effort invested in this work will pay off when you have strong and shared mental models of what teachers need to know, do and care about to have the greatest impact on the learners in their care.

> ## Questions for reflection
> - How well do you understand the evidence-informed pedagogical approaches described in this chapter? Could you explain them easily to a colleague? And how might this understanding influence the priorities you set for teacher development and classroom practice in your school?
> - What can you do to focus your colleagues' attention on one pedagogical approach without inadvertently neglecting the others? How can you ensure a holistic and interconnected approach to teaching and learning?
> - In what ways could you enhance the professional development systems in your school to address individual teacher needs, while fostering collective expertise and aligning with the principles of adaptive expertise?

References

Blazar D and Kraft MA (2015) Exploring mechanisms of effective teacher coaching. *Educational Evaluation and Policy Analysis* 37(4): 542–566.

Blazar D, McNamara D and Blue G (2021) Instructional coaching personnel and program scalability. *EdWorkingPaper* no. 21-499. Available at: https://files.eric.ed.gov/fulltext/ED616777.pdf (accessed 29 November 2024).

Coe R (2013) *Improving Education: A triumph of hope over experience.* Centre for Evaluation and Monitoring. Available at: http://eachandeverydog.net/wp-content/uploads/2015/05/ImprovingEducation2013.pdf (accessed 29 November 2024).

Coe R (2014) Classroom observation: It's harder than you think. In: *Cambridge CEM Blog.* Available at: https://cem.org/blog/classroom-observation (accessed 29 November 2024).

Coe R, Rauch C, Kime S et al. (2020) *Great Teaching Toolkit: Evidence Review.* Available at: https://cambridgeinternational.org/Images/584543-great-teaching-toolkit-evidence-review.pdf (accessed 29 November 2024).

Goldhaber D, Krieg J and Theobald R (2020) Effective like me? Does having a more productive mentor improve the productivity of mentees? *Labour Economics* 63: 101792.

Hattie J (2003) Teachers Make a Difference: What is the research evidence? In: *ACER Research Conference*, Melbourne, Australia, October 2003. Available at: https://research.acer.edu.au/cgi/viewcontent.cgi?article=1003&context=research_conference_2003 (accessed 29 November 2024).

Kern L and Clemens, NH (2007) Antecedent strategies to promote appropriate classroom behavior. *Psychology in the Schools* 44(1): 65–75.

Kraft MA, Blazar D and Hogan D (2018) The effect of teacher coaching on instruction and achievement: A meta-analysis of the causal evidence. *Review of Educational Research* 88(4): 547–588.

Lin X, Schwartz DL and Bransford J (2007) Intercultural adaptive expertise: Explicit and implicit lessons from Dr Hatano. *Human Development* 50(1): 65–72.

CHAPTER 3

Leading curriculum

Grace Healy, IOE – *Faculty of Education and Society, University College London, UK; Department of Education, University of Oxford, UK; David Ross Education Trust, UK*

This chapter will consider:
- the big ideas from research, theory and evidence that leaders should be aware of in order to lead curriculum effectively
- how leaders can utilise the curriculum to deliver strong outcomes for all, address inequality and promote inclusion.

What is curriculum?

For the purposes of this chapter, curriculum is considered as 'the multi-layered social practices, including infrastructure, pedagogy and assessment, through which education is structured, enacted and evaluated' (Priestley, 2019). As a leader, you hold responsibility for processes and systems that contribute to these social practices, such as:

- the time you give to teachers to select knowledge and pedagogical approaches
- the professional development that you establish to support teachers' curriculum work
- how you approach the timetabling of the curriculum
- how you consider local context and students' needs as the curriculum is shaped in your setting.

Curriculum is a dynamic and contextual process shaped by the complex interplay of policy, context and teacher agency (Ball et al., 2012).

This chapter will focus on the following key considerations drawn from research and theory for leading curriculum:

1. Curriculum coherence
2. Teachers' intellectual work
3. Senior curriculum leadership
4. Addressing inequality and promoting inclusion.

Curriculum coherence

Research highlights the importance of alignment between aims, content, pedagogy and assessment, so that all aspects of the curriculum work together towards clear educational goals. Bernstein (1996), for example, introduced the pedagogic device, a theoretical framework that describes the translation of knowledge into pedagogical communication. In your own context, you have some scope to ensure this curriculum coherence. However, some curriculum decisions are taken at the national level.
At the time of writing, the Department for Education has launched its *Curriculum and Assessment Review* (DfE, 2024), signalling changes to national curriculum policy in England. There are debates that rest on the false dichotomy of knowledge *versus* skills, but each subject needs to engage with *both* knowledge and skills, and knowledge and skills should both be considered as types of knowledge (Winch, 2013). There are also various ways to consider what education is for. Biesta (2010) draws on the three domains of:

- qualification – provision of necessary 'knowledge, skills and understandings' (p. 19)
- socialisation – enabling students to 'become part of particular social, cultural and political "orders"' (p. 20)
- subjectification – enabling students to 'become more autonomous and independent in their thinking and acting' (p. 21).

A question you might ask yourself is: 'What counts as an educated 19-year-old in this day and age?' (Pring, 2013, p. 8). You might consider what your school's contribution to this is: what do you expect students to know and do in each subject or by each phase?

There are various approaches to the organisation of the curriculum, including knowledge progression and sequencing of curricula content. For example, Bruner's (1960, p. 12) spiral curriculum is a model that is designed to 'revisit … basic ideas repeatedly, building upon them until the student has grasped the full formal apparatus that goes with them'. Knowledge progression also differs between subjects depending on the structure of knowledge within these domains. For example, maths and science come from disciplines that have hierarchical knowledge structures, whereas English literature, geography and history have horizontal knowledge structures (Bernstein, 1999). At a curriculum planning level, this means that in some subjects, such as maths, there is a logical order in which concepts are sequenced. For example, you would ensure that students master addition as a prerequisite to understanding multiplication. Whereas in other subjects, there are multiple ways to sequence curricula content and concepts.

As discussed in the first chapter, as a leader you can enable curricula coherence across subjects to strengthen and enrich students' educational experience, while still recognising the distinctive contribution of each subject. There are some aspects of the curriculum that are particularly well suited to being taught in such a way. We can now consider three such examples.

Oracy and literacy

Students' oracy and literacy are fundamental in enabling students to access learning across all subjects, and all subjects play a distinctive role in contributing to the development of oracy and literacy. There are generic and subject-specific components to both oracy and literacy (Quigley and Coleman, 2018; Moorghen, 2023). As a school leader, you will be considering what needs to be consistent (set out as a whole-school approach) and how you enable subject-specific support. For example:

- Do you have a shared language for teachers and students to talk about oracy and literacy across the whole curriculum?
- How do you ensure that 'training related to literacy prioritises subject specificity over general approaches' (Quigley and Coleman, 2018, p. 6)?
- As part of curriculum planning, how do you ensure that teachers consider explicitly what words and phrases will be taught?

Careers

Linking curriculum learning to careers is part of the Gatsby Benchmarks for secondary schools and colleges in England. As part of the Gatsby Benchmarks that were updated in 2024, the criteria state that 'every year, in every subject, every pupil should have opportunities to learn how the knowledge and skills developed in that subject ... [help] people to gain entry to, and be more effective workers within, a wide range of careers' (The Gatsby Charitable Foundation, 2024, p. 30). Careers input should be included in staff development for teachers, including having careers advisors or careers leaders working with teachers based on local labour market information.

Climate change and sustainability

Surveys of teachers (across primary and secondary phases) and students (from Key Stage 3) in England have identified that teachers and students alike want the opportunity to be able to teach and learn about climate change and sustainability across a greater range of subjects (Greer et al., 2023; Walshe et al., 2024). While teachers can embed climate change and sustainability in their subject curricula, how do you strategically support teachers' awareness of students' prior knowledge and future learning for other subjects? Alongside supporting this join-up across subject curricula, you have the greatest agency to address tensions between what is taught in the curriculum and practices related to sustainability within the school. Students can perceive that schools are not acting in sustainable ways, and this can be challenging for teachers to deal with in the classroom (Dave and Hoath, 2024). By 2025, 'all education settings will have nominated a sustainability lead and put in place a climate action plan' (DfE, 2023). How will you formalise how curricula coherence might be developed in connection with sustainability practices in your school(s)?

Teachers' intellectual work

Young and Muller (2010) offer three scenarios for the future of education and how knowledge is viewed within school subjects in each of these scenarios (see **Table 3.1**). As part of a 'Future 3' curriculum scenario, where knowledge is seen to be dynamic, there are implicit demands on teachers to sustain their own knowledge of the parent discipline in order to recontextualise knowledge for students (Young and Muller, 2010). While 'the majority of secondary teachers have a particular specialism in one subject discipline, on the basis of a single epistemological understanding of what knowledge is' (Puttick, Elliott and Ingram, 2024, p. 15), primary teachers have more complex relationships to the range of subjects that they teach.

Future scenario	View of knowledge	Implication for school subject
Future 1	Under-socialised knowledge for the powerful	Elitist – subject boundaries are fixed and maintained. Knowledge is fixed and backward looking.
Future 2	Over-socialised knowledge lacks power	Subject boundaries are removed. Generic learning outcomes, such as skills, become the aim – a turn away from knowledge.
Future 3	Social realist powerful knowledge	Subject knowledge boundaries are maintained but also crossed for the creation and acquisition of new knowledge. Subject knowledge is dynamic and forward looking.

Table 3.1: Three futures for subject knowledge (Mitchell, 2017, p. 68, adapted from Young and Muller, 2010).

In secondary schools, how do you enable teachers to remain connected to their subject's parent discipline, in order to understand contemporary subject debates rather than seeing subject knowledge as something that can be 'auditable' (Ellis, 2007, p. 164)? This requires thinking about the time and space you give to subject teachers to (1) engage with disciplinary and subject education scholarship to sustain their subject expertise, (2) situate their own practice among other subject specialists to illuminate other approaches to curriculum development, and (3) support critical engagement with how their subject is represented within curriculum policy. For example, is subject department time dedicated to this? Are your subject departments funded to access subject association journals and attend subject-specific professional development (PD)? Do you give professional recognition to teachers who contribute to their national subject communities? Professional practice feeds some subjects and, therefore, subject teachers benefit from sustaining their own practice (e.g. as artists and musicians) or engaging with forms of professional practice related to their subject area. Do you recognise this form of development within PD and performance management processes?

Senior curriculum leadership

As a leader, you are responsible for establishing processes that assure the scope and sequencing of the curriculum in each subject is fit for purpose (intent), and that there is fidelity to that intent across year groups and by all teachers (implementation). How do you ensure that the scope and sequencing of each subject's curriculum provides all students with a secure and extensive understanding of the subject, while also preparing those who pursue the subject at the examination level with a strong foundation?

Assessment and feedback are drivers of learning that should be integrated with curriculum planning (Black and Wiliam, 1998; Hattie, 2009). What is formative and summative assessment telling you about how well students are learning the curriculum? How do you ensure that this informs curriculum planning and teaching? Teachers should be given enough time after summative assessments to address how knowledge and skills that have not been secured by all will be addressed through the curriculum. As summative assessment data is a lagged measure, data should also be drawn from other indicators, such as attendance data, behaviour data and homework completion.

Professional dialogue with subject leaders and teachers is vital to understand and evaluate the implementation of subject curricula, and helps to ensure that you do not rely on proxies such as lesson observations and curriculum documentation, which can conceal teachers' intellectual work (Healy, 2024). The knowledge base for leading curriculum requires engagement in subject community discourse and practice across a broad range of subjects. National subject associations and journals often provide a way for those who line-manage subject areas beyond their own expertise to explore this knowledge base. Subject leaders need the expertise to design, refine and evaluate the curriculum across year groups, and you hold responsibility for ensuring that they have the required resources and expertise to undertake these roles.

Teachers interpret and enact the curriculum, and use their subject expertise to adapt and teach it effectively for a particular set of students.

Lambert (2018) outlines the following central questions that need to be understood and addressed by teachers as they enact the curriculum:

- 'Who are the students?

  (What is their prior experience and knowledge? What are their aspirations?)
- Why teach this subject?
  (How does it justify curriculum space? What is its educational value?)
- What should be taught?
  (On what basis do we select what to teach? How is this sequenced?)
- How do we best teach this subject?
  (What pedagogic approaches are suited to serving the purposes identified above?)' (Lambert, 2018, p. 367).

For many teachers, their initial teacher education (ITE) will provide them with the foundations to begin to understand and then be able to address these questions, and they will then strengthen this understanding throughout their careers. Caldwell et al. (2021) highlight how primary teachers do not always gain strong underpinnings in all subjects, especially foundation subjects, such as art, computing, geography, history and physical education. In the secondary phase, you may also need to consider the support you can give to those teaching beyond their main subject specialism.

Addressing inequality and promoting inclusion

As a school leader, ideally, you want to utilise the curriculum strategically to deliver strong outcomes, address inequality and promote inclusion by ensuring it reflects diverse perspectives and provides flexible pathways to meet the needs of all learners. High-quality teaching, supported by professional development, can emphasise inclusive pedagogies and appropriate adaptive teaching and scaffolding. For example, having systems and processes in place to ensure that all teachers are aware of, and can accurately assess, students' reading ages will equip them to effectively support students' reading in their lessons. As a leader, you can use data to identify attainment gaps and inform targeted interventions that address any disparities. Targeted support ensures equitable access to resources and opportunities for students facing systemic barriers (e.g. students who are persistently absent, students who are young carers). For example, additional reading support can be provided for students whose parents/carers are not able to listen to them read at home, or alternatives to revision interventions outside school hours can be made available for students who are young carers and cannot stay at the end of the school day.

Promoting inclusion and valuing diversity are fundamental aspects of developing and evaluating the scope (breadth and depth) and rigour of all subject curricula across all phases. The 'Lit in Colour' report (Elliott et al., 2021) exemplifies the urgency of this curriculum- and teacher-development work within the sector for the subject of English literature. It indicates that 'there is systematic underrepresentation of writers of colour in our curriculum' (p. 60), and the authors recommend 'support for diversification of the curriculum in terms of planning time; financial resources to buy books; readiness to speak with parents' (p. 61). Across all subjects, curriculum development that enables inclusivity and diversity to be addressed in meaningful ways requires a sustained approach to teacher development, financial support for teacher and student resources, and mechanisms for involving the wider school community. The 'Inquiry on equity in STEM education' report (APPG on Diversity and Inclusion in STEM, 2020, p. 27) identified that 'the curriculum itself and associated teaching resources often focus too heavily on male role models and … perpetuate unhelpful stereotypes in relation to STEM'. How can you ensure that, across all subjects, you think about representation within the curriculum? For example, in mathematics, do teachers include 'diverse mathematicians, historical perspectives, and mathematical contributions from various cultural and social backgrounds … [that help] students see themselves reflected in the subject' (AMSP, 2024)?

Conclusion

Leading curriculum is a dynamic and multi-faceted endeavour that requires balancing national policy demands, local contexts and the needs of students, while fostering teacher agency and professional expertise. As a leader, your role is not only to oversee the systems and processes that underpin curriculum design and teaching, but also to cultivate a culture wherein all stakeholders – teachers, students, parents and the wider school community – are empowered to engage meaningfully with the curriculum. As you navigate the complexities of curriculum leadership, consider the central question raised earlier: 'What counts as an educated 19-year-old in this day and age?' By keeping this question at the heart of your decisions, you can ensure that your curriculum reflects contemporary aspirations, challenges and opportunities, equipping students not only for academic success but also for meaningful and fulfilling lives.

> ## Questions for reflection
> - As a school leader, do you know how the structure of knowledge influences each subject's curriculum sequencing?
> - How do you capture how PD contributes to effective implementation of the curriculum? What forms of data do you use to evaluate the implementation of the curriculum?
> - How can you ensure that all students feel represented within the curriculum?

References

Advanced Mathematics Support Programme (AMSP) (n.d.) *Diversifying the curriculum*. Available at: https://amsp.org.uk/teachers/equity-diversity-and-inclusion/diversifying-the-curriculum (accessed 30 November 2024).

All-Party Parliamentary Group (APPG) on Diversity and Inclusion in STEM (2020) *Inquiry on Equity in STEM education: Final report*. Available at: https://britishscienceassociation.org/equity-in-stem-education (accessed 30 November 2024).

Ball SJ, Maguire M and Braun A (2012) *How Schools Do Policy: Policy Enactments in Secondary Schools*. Abingdon: Routledge.

Bernstein B (1996) *Pedagogy, Symbolic Control, and Identity: Theory, Research, Critique*. London: Taylor Francis.

Bernstein B (1999) Vertical and Horizontal Discourse: an essay. *British Journal of Sociology of Education* 20(2): 157–173.

Biesta GJ (2010) *Good Education in an Age of Measurement: Ethics, Politics, Democracy*. Abingdon: Routledge.

Black P and Wiliam D (1998) Inside the black box: Raising standards through classroom assessment. *Phi Delta Kappan* 80(2): 139–148.

Bruner JS (1960) *The Process of Education*. Cambridge, MA: Harvard University Press.

Caldwell H, Whewell E, Bracey P et al. (2021) Teaching on insecure foundations? Pre-service teachers in England's perceptions of the wider curriculum subjects in primary schools. *Cambridge Journal of Education* 51(2): 231–246.

Dave H and Hoath L (2024) The criticality of sensemaking in climate change education: Closing the gap between information gathering and curriculum making in schools. *The Curriculum Journal* 35(1): 129–132.

Department for Education (DfE) (2023) *Sustainability and climate change strategy: A strategy for the education and children's services systems.* Available at: https://gov.uk/government/publications/sustainability-and-climate-change-strategy/9317e6ed-6c80-4eb9-be6d-3fcb1f232f3a (accessed 19 October 2024).

Department for Education (DfE) (2024) *Curriculum and assessment review.* Available at: https://gov.uk/government/groups/curriculum-and-assessment-review (accessed 19 October 2024).

Elliott V, Nelson-Addy L, Chantiluke R et al. (2021) *Lit in colour: Diversity in literature in English schools.* Penguin and Runnymede Trust. Available at: https://litincolour.penguin.co.uk/assets/Lit-in-Colour-research-report.pdf (accessed 17 December 2024)

Ellis V (2007) *Subject Knowledge and Teacher Education: The Development of Beginning Teachers' Thinking.* London: Continuum Studies in Education.

Greer K, Sheldrake R, Rushton E et al. (2023) *Teaching climate change and sustainability: A survey of teachers in England.* University College London. Available at: https://discovery.ucl.ac.uk/id/eprint/10173208/ (accessed 19 October 2024).

Hattie J (2009) *Visible Learning: A Synthesis of Over 800 Meta-Analyses Relating to Achievement.* London: Routledge.

Healy G (2024) *Rendering visible teachers' intellectual work: An examination of the recontextualisation of knowledge through geography teachers' professional practice.* PhD thesis, University College London. Available at: https://discovery.ucl.ac.uk/id/eprint/10187603/ (accessed 19 October 2024).

Lambert D (2018) Teaching as a research-engaged profession: Uncovering a blind spot and revealing new possibilities. *London Review of Education* 16(3): 357–370.

Mitchell D (2017) *Geography curriculum making in changing times.* PhD thesis, University College London. Available at: https://discovery.ucl.ac.uk/id/eprint/1576544/ (accessed 17 December 2024).

Moorghen A (2023) Is every teacher a teacher of oracy? *English: Journal of the English Association* 72(278): 126–130.

Priestley M (2019) Curriculum: Concepts and approaches. Available at: https://mrpriestley.wordpress.com/2019/01/04/curriculum-concepts-and-approaches/ (accessed 30 November 2024).

Pring R (2013) What counts as an educated 19-year-old in this day and age? *Teachers College Record* 115(13): 18–21.

Puttick S, Elliott V and Ingram J (2024) *Knowledge: Keywords in Teacher Education.* London: Bloomsbury.

Quigley A and Coleman R (2018) *Improving literacy in secondary schools: Guidance report.* Education Endowment Foundation. Available at: https://educationendowmentfoundation.org.uk/education-evidence/guidance-reports/literacy-ks3-ks4 (accessed 17 December 2024).

The Gatsby Charitable Foundation (2024) *Good career guidance: The next 10 years.* Available at: https://gatsbybenchmarks.org.uk/app/uploads/2024/11/good-career-guidance-the-next-10-years-report.pdf (accessed 17 December 2024).

Walshe N, Sheldrake R, Healy G et al. (2024) *Climate change and sustainability education: A survey of students in England.* University College London. Available at: https://discovery.ucl.ac.uk/id/eprint/10195286/ (accessed 19 October 2024).

Winch C (2013) Curriculum design and epistemic ascent. *Journal of Philosophy of Education* 47(1): 28–146.

Young M and Muller J (2010) Three educational scenarios for the future: Lessons from the sociology of knowledge. *European Journal of Education* 45(1): 11–26.

CHAPTER 4

Purposeful assessment

Corinne Settle, *Senior Educational Lead for Embedding Formative Assessment, The Schools, Students and Teachers Network (SSAT), UK*

This chapter will consider:
- the importance of building teacher expertise around formative assessment
- the importance of teacher and leader assessment literacy
- how to utilise assessment purposefully
- cautions around high-stakes accountability.

> 'Assessment should be the servant, not the master, of the learning.' (Wiliam, 2014, p. 2)

Assessment can take many forms, but for the purposes of this chapter, we will define the predominant two types. Formative assessment can be defined as a tool for making inferences about student learning, informing teaching strategies and guiding instructional decisions (adapted from Cizek and Lim, 2023). On the other hand, summative assessment is used to summarise learning that has taken place, focusing more on attainment and tracking progress after particular periods of time (National Foundation for Educational Research, nd). Both types of assessment can be used to evaluate student progress, and both can inform teaching strategies and areas for development of learning. However, they are applied in different ways for different purposes, according to the needs of learners, teachers and schools. Therefore, assessment has three core purposes (Earl, 2013):

1. to improve learning

2. to inform classroom teaching

3. to support school-level decision-making.

The purpose of assessment

In examining our assumptions and beliefs around the purposes of assessment, we might find that we need to take a more nuanced and equitable approach to assessing our students, in order to cater for the diverse needs of all learners. A significant portion of students – around a third – do not achieve at least a grade 4 standard pass in GCSE English and maths after 12 years of schooling (Association of School and College Leaders, 2019). This raises questions around assessment practices and policies and whether or not these are fit for the purpose of supporting all learners to progress. For example, the ASCL's (2019) 'The forgotten third' report states that even upon arriving at (both primary and secondary) school, students from lower-income backgrounds are already behind their more affluent peers in terms of vocabulary, which puts them at a significant disadvantage when it comes to being assessed, due to the fact that 'current GCSEs in all subjects demand a much broader vocabulary than previous specifications' (ASCL, 2019, p. 17). This disparity therefore begins long before students arrive in the classroom, as (for some) conversations and introductions to reading start at home during the Early Years phase. This is reflected in a report by The Sutton Trust (2024), which argues for a core entitlement of 20 hours per week in early education for all two-, three- and four-year-olds, in order to address this gap.

The Education Endowment Foundation's (EEF) *Teaching and Learning Toolkit* (EEF, 2018a) supports formative assessment as a 'best bet' for closing the gap between high-achieving and underachieving students. Five of the highest potential impact strands are encompassed in formative assessment: metacognition and self-regulation; oral language interventions; feedback; collaborative learning and peer tutoring.

However, it is important to consider that there has been some critique around the 'deficit' framing of the vocabulary gap (Cushing, 2024). Research has cautioned us not to perceive students who experience 'social disadvantage' as a homogenous group – indeed, not all students who grow up in areas of social deprivation will have poor language development (Schofield, 2023). This is where a deep understanding of the specific context of your school and its learners' individual needs is important.

In 2014, the DfE granted schools autonomy to design their own assessment systems, aiming to better meet students' needs. While high-stakes accountability aims to ensure educational standards, it carries inherent risks, particularly for learners. For example, East Asian education systems are often lauded for their top rankings in international testing, but these systems have also been criticised for eroding student confidence and attitudes, while diminishing their interest in subjects such as maths, science and reading (Zhao, 2016) – effects that may not feel unfamiliar to teachers in the UK (Chollet et al., 2024). This highlights a need for a more balanced approach to summative methods of assessment more generally. Context is important here too, and it has been suggested that tailored observation tools are a more useful, sympathetic and context-specific way in which to improve the quality of data for teacher accountability (Hopfenbeck, 2017), while balancing high-stakes testing with assessments that support students' overall confidence, interest and wellbeing.

This is not to say that summative assessment is unnecessary or unimportant. As a school leader, you need to be able to monitor learner progress towards overall goals. But, as leaders, we would do well to honestly confront the fact that such monitoring may have little impact on actual achievement. Instead, a focus on improving lesson-by-lesson formative assessment in the classroom has the potential to yield significant improvements in student attainment (EEF, 2018b).

Rather than the traditional 'data-driven decision-making', the future of assessment calls for 'decision-driven data collection' (Wiliam et al., 2024, p. 5). By focusing on the decisions that need to be made, as a leader you will be in a better position to gather the right amount of relevant data in ways that actually benefit learners, teachers and your school. Every interaction with a student is a potential assessment opportunity, providing insights into learning and helping teachers to adapt their instruction. As Coe (2018) writes, 'Assessment must contain information. In practice, that means it could surprise you: it could tell you something you don't already know.' Assessment is effective communication between teaching and learning, offering teachers actionable information about students' understanding and needs. The true purpose of assessment lies in its value to *improve* learning.

From formative intention to formative action

In 2002, the Assessment Reform Group (Broadfoot et al., 2002) identified 10 research-based principles for effective assessment for learning (AfL):

1. Assessment should be part of effective planning of teaching and learning.
2. It should focus on how students learn.
3. It should be central to classroom practice.
4. It should be a key professional skill for teachers.
5. It should be sensitive and constructive, because any assessment has an emotional impact.
6. It should take into account the importance of learning motivation.
7. It should promote commitment to learning goals and a shared understanding of the assessment criteria.
8. Learners should receive constructive guidance about how to improve.
9. It should develop learners' capacity for self-assessment so that they can become reflective and self-managing.
10. It should recognise the full range of achievements of all learners.

The term 'assessment for learning' (AfL), promoted by the Assessment Reform Group (ARG), is a statement about the purpose of assessment rather than a descriptor of its role in student learning (Wiliam et al., 2024). It is an intentional phrase that must be backed by action and strategies in order to move learning forward and to avoid a superficial focus on teacher-led techniques.

An assessment functions formatively to the extent that evidence about student achievement is elicited, interpreted and used by teachers or students to make decisions about the next steps in instruction that are likely to be better – or better founded – than the decisions that they would have taken in the absence of that elicited evidence (Black and Wiliam, 2009). Or, in short: 'Better Evidence, Better Decisions, Better Learning' (Wiliam et al., 2024).

The evidence base for formative assessment spans four decades, with numerous studies and meta-analyses demonstrating its potential significant impact. Wisniewski et al.'s (2020) recent meta-analysis, showing an average effect size of 0.5, reinforces its potential to enhance student learning, and Black and Wiliam's foundational review (1998) remains pivotal, continuing to shape and influence research.

Studies have explored how formative assessment impacts not only learning but also student behaviour and motivation. A study by the EEF on the Schools, Students and Teachers Network (SSAT) (nd) Embedding Formative Assessment (EFA) programme showed a significant impact of the programme on GCSE outcomes, equivalent to two additional months of progress in students' Attainment 8 GCSE scores (EEF, 2018b). This trial remains the only whole-school programme proven to impact GCSE results, demonstrating the power of well-implemented formative assessment through professional learning communities (PLCs) as a vehicle for teacher and school change. PLCs provide a collaborative and supportive space for groups of eight to 14 teachers to meet in structured workshops. There are eight workshops per year over two years, which follow a signature pedagogy of deliberate practice and peer feedback.

Learner motivation and engagement

Formative assessment is a pedagogy of engagement and responsiveness. No child should go through a school day contributing little to their learning. There are many reasons why a learner may be disengaged, passive or opting out of learning. As teachers, we don't know what we don't know, and we don't know what our students know. Effective formative assessment allows teachers to monitor students' development and respond to individual needs, which can enhance school connectedness and reduce behaviour problems (Oates, 2024).

The most overlooked principles of assessment recognised by the ARG are those that focus on the impact on the learner. This is often due to accountability measures (Hutchings, 2015). Feedback, identified by the EEF as having the highest potential for additional progress (up to six months), should be aimed at motivating students and fostering a belief in their ability to improve (EEF, 2021; Beckmann et al., 2009). Research by Yeager et al. (2014) indicates that students are more likely to act on feedback if they believe that they can meet high standards and achieve success.

However, getting this kind of feedback right is difficult. Kluger and DeNisi (1996) found that only two out of eight possible outcomes from feedback are positive: increased effort and increased aspiration. Some of the potential negative effects of feedback include a reduction in effort and/or aspiration, abandoning the goal (because it is too hard or too easy) or rejecting the feedback.

It is important to note that feedback and marking are not the same thing. Feedback can be verbal, non-verbal or written, and the EEF's (2021) 'Teacher feedback to improve student learning' report highlights that oral feedback may have a slightly more positive effect than written feedback. The foundation for getting feedback right is the relationship between learner and teacher, with feedback focusing on task, subject and self-regulation strategies. For feedback to be effective, it must focus on improving the learner, not just the piece of work at hand, and should create more work for the learner than for the teacher (Hattie and Timperley, 2007).

Grading or levelling students as part of feedback can have negative effects on learning, motivation and achievement (Kluger and DeNisi, 1996; Black and Wiliam, 1998). Phrases such as 'working towards' or 'making expected progress' can be equally value-laden and may halt learning. Judgements should be given as infrequently as possible.

Learner motivation, or the lack of it, can be effectively addressed through formative assessment strategies. Eliciting evidence of learning techniques that prevent students from opting out ensures that every learner is engaged and has the opportunity to experience success. This approach allows teachers to respond to individual learner needs, fostering a belief in students that they can succeed. As confidence builds, motivation grows, creating a positive spiral where increased motivation leads to greater success (Muijs, 2022).

Peer- and self-assessment, often overlooked in efforts to improve teacher responsiveness, play a crucial role in this process. When students assess their peers' work, they are forced to internalise success criteria in a less emotionally charged context, making it easier to understand what constitutes quality work. As a result, their performance often improves after providing feedback to others. This reflective process not only clarifies expectations but also enhances students' understanding of their work.

Empowering learners to actively participate in assessment helps them to become effective, confident and self-regulated. This is essential for fostering lifelong learners in an ever-evolving world, where the ability to adapt and manage one's learning is increasingly important.

The importance of assessment literacy

Effective assessment depends on the assessment literacy of teachers and leaders, enabling them to interpret data accurately and use it to drive decisions that improve teaching and learning (Christodoulou, 2017; Wiliam, 2014). Leaders must ensure that assessments are purposeful and provide reliable insights into student understanding and needs.

Supporting teachers in avoiding assessment pitfalls is critical. For example, using hinge questions and analysing patterns across multiple assessments helps to identify misconceptions and track progress without relying on superficial indicators like student engagement (Coe, 2013). High-quality formative assessments embedded in lessons enable real-time instructional adjustments (Wiliam et al., 2024), while externally validated summative resources enhance reliability (Hattie and Timperley, 2007).

Leaders play a key role in fostering the assessment literacy of teachers by providing streamlined systems and professional development focused on efficient, evidence-based practices (Gibson et al., 2015).

Practical actions for leaders to improve assessment literacy include:

- building expertise using current research and evidenced-based approaches
- evaluating and updating school-wide assessment approaches, identifying clear purposes and principles to enhance their impact on learners
- providing professional development to build shared expertise, with reflection on knowledge and skills
- collaborating and reflecting on assessment design to apply principles through co-construction and moderation of assessments and classroom techniques.

Implementing formative assessment practices

To implement formative assessment effectively, consider the following actions:

1. **Audit your curriculum for slack:** A curriculum built solely on the foundation of content without pedagogy often results in lessons rammed with content and no slack to collect better evidence and, most importantly, to respond to the evidence collected. If the evidence collected doesn't lead to action, then the technique, no matter how well performed, has no value. Teachers need time to implement formative assessment within lessons (Wiliam, in Lough, 2020).

2. **Plan professional development that supports habit change:** Teaching practices are often deeply ingrained and habitual. To change them, teachers need to identify triggers and practise improved responses repeatedly (Hobbiss et al., 2020). This is why the Embedding Formative Assessment programme focuses on choice, flexibility, small steps, accountability and support through PLCs (Wiliam and Leahy, 2014). A collaborative, structured process enables habit change.

3. **Reframe assessment:** Create a culture where assessment is seen by teachers and students as a tool for learning rather than a mechanism of judgement.

Conclusion

Purposeful assessment is a critical component of effective teaching and learning. By building teacher and leader expertise in assessment literacy and practice, we can ensure that assessments not only provide evidence of student progress but actively enhance it. Assessment is a continuous process in the classroom; it is not merely *for* learning – it *is* learning. This daily practice must sit within a wider formative and summative assessment system that is carefully designed to reflect student learning without undermining it. Every classroom assessment should be designed to improve both learning and the learner, fostering a supportive environment that drives engagement, motivation and success.

LEADERSHIP INSIGHT

Building a shared understanding of assessment with parents and students

*Claire Badger, Assistant Head, Teaching and Learning,
Godolphin and Latymer School, UK*

At Godolphin and Latymer School in London, leaders and teachers work together to communicate clear messages about assessment to students and their parents, helping to build a collective understanding of the purpose and role of assessment in education. Our students are incredibly motivated and want to achieve well, but this can result in them placing too much emphasis on the outcome of different assessments taken throughout the school year, often resulting in markedly increased stress and anxiety around upcoming tests.

With this in mind, one of the key messages we share is that the only *summative* assessments students take are formal, end-of-key-stage examinations and that any other assessment should be seen as *formative* – i.e. an opportunity to give students and their teachers useful information that can be acted on. For these internal assessments, teachers avoid placing too much emphasis on marks and grades and instead focus on providing useful feedback for students; whole-class feedback approaches are encouraged, as are assessment follow-up tasks which allow students to make their own corrections and improvements.

Talking to students about the difference between 'learning' and 'performance' zones (Briceno, 2016) has been a valuable way of framing this. We contextualise assessments as being part of the learning zone where mistakes are expected to happen; how you act on the feedback you are given is the most important thing. Daisy Christodoulou (2017) shares a marathon analogy which has proved useful in helping to build staff and student understanding around our approach. Christodoulou argues that you wouldn't prepare for a marathon by running lots of marathons, and in the same way, solely focusing on lots of high-stakes past papers isn't the best way of helping students prepare for exams. Asking students to consider learning and performance zones in other areas of their life is also a good way to broaden their thinking.

Students have also told us that when it comes to assessments, they sometimes worry because they don't want to let their parents down. In an effort to alleviate this, we have also sought to build parental understanding around the purpose of assessment, by holding online talks to explain the context of educational assessment in England and some of the associated complexities. Our main message to parents is that rather than asking their child what mark they achieved in a particular assessment, they should instead ask what they learnt from the process.

> Ensuring that the whole community has a better understanding of the difference between summative and formative assessment has played an essential role in shifting mindsets. With similar messages coming from teachers *and* parents, students are able to approach internal assessments in a more measured fashion and, as a result, learn much more from the experience.
>
> Claire Badger was awarded Chartered Teacher (Leadership) Status in 2021.

Questions for reflection

- How do the teachers in your setting respond to different levels of accountability that can be placed on assessments?
- What is the culture of assessment in your setting? Are teachers regularly encouraged to actively reflect on the purposes of their assessment practices?
- In what ways are the teachers in your setting supported to build their expertise around assessment?

References

ASCL (2019) *The Forgotten Third: Final report of the Commission of Inquiry.* Available at: https://ascl.org.uk/ASCL/media/ASCL/Our%20view/Campaigns/The-Forgotten-Third_full-report.pdf (accessed 11 September 2024).

Beckmann N, Beckmann JF and Elliot JG (2009) Self-confidence and performance goal orientation interactively predict performance in a reasoning test with accuracy feedback. *Learning and Individual Differences* 10(2): 277–282.

Black P and Wiliam D (1998) Assessment and classroom learning. *Assessment in Education: Principles, Policy and Practice* 5(1): 7–74.

Black P and Wiliam D (2009) Developing the theory of formative assessment. *Educational Assessment, Evaluation and Accountability* 21(1): 5–31.

Briceno E (2016) How to get better at the things you care about. *TED,* November 2016. Available at: https://ted.com/talks/eduardo_briceno_how_to_get_better_at_the_things_you_care_about?subtitle=en (accessed 21 November 2024).

Broadfoot PM, Daugherty R, Gardner J et al. (2002) *Assessment for Learning: 10 principles: Research-based principles to guide classroom practice.* Assessment Reform Group. Available at: https://storre.stir.ac.uk/bitstream/1893/32458/1/Assessment%20for%20learning%2010%20principles%202002.pdf (accessed 26 November 2024).

Chollet D, Turner A, Marquez J et al. (2024) *The Good Childhood Report 2024*. The Children's Society. Available at: https://childrenssociety.org.uk/sites/default/files/2024-08/Good%20Childhood%20Report-Main-Report.pdf (accessed 26 November 2024).

Christodoulou D (2017) *Making Good Progress: The future of assessment for learning*. Oxford: Oxford University Press.

Cizek GJ and Lim SN (2023) *Formative assessment: An overview of history, theory and application*. In: Tierney RJ, Rizvi F and Ercikan K (eds) *International Encyclopaedia of Education*, 4th ed. Amsterdam: Elsevier Science, pp. 1–9.

Coe R (2013) *Improving education: A triumph of hope over experience*. Durham University. https://f.hubspotusercontent30.net/hubfs/5191137/attachments/publications/ImprovingEducation2013.pdf (accessed 3 December 2024).

Coe R (2018) *But that is NOT AN ASSESSMENT!* Cambridge Centre for Evaluation and Monitoring. Available at: https://cem.org/blog/but-that-is-not-an-assessment (accessed 3 December 2024).

Cushing I (2024) Social (in)justice and the deficit foundations of oracy. *Oxford Review of Education* 1–18.

Earl L (2013) *Assessment as Learning: Using Classroom Assessment to Maximise Student Learning*, 2nd ed. Thousand Oaks, CA: Corwin Press.

Education Endowment Foundation (EEF) (2018a) *Teaching and Learning Toolkit*. Available at: https://educationendowmentfoundation.org.uk/evidence-summaries/teaching-learning-toolkit/ (accessed 11 September 2024).

Education Endowment Foundation (EEF) (2018b) *Embedding Formative Assessment: Evaluation report and executive summary*. Available at: https://educationendowmentfoundation.org.uk/projects-and-evaluation/projects/embedding-formative-assessment (accessed 4 November 2024).

Education Endowment Foundation (EEF) (2021) *Teacher Feedback to Improve Pupil Learning*. Available at: https://educationendowmentfoundation.org.uk/education-evidence/guidance-reports/feedback (accessed 11 September 2024).

Gibson S, Oliver L and Dennison R (2015) *Workload Challenge: Analysis of teacher consultation responses*. Department for Education. Available at: https://assets.publishing.service.gov.uk/government/uploads/system/uploads/attachment_data/file/401406/RR445_-_Workload_Challenge_-_Analysis_of_teacher_consultation_responses_FINAL.pdf (accessed 26 November 2024).

Hattie J and Timperley H (2007) The power of feedback. *Review of Educational Research* 77(1): 81–112.

Hobbiss M, Sims S and Allen R (2020) Habit formation limits growth in teacher effectiveness: A review of converging evidence from neuroscience and social science. *Review of Education* 9(1): 3–23.

Hopfenbeck TN (2017) Balancing the challenges of high-stakes testing, accountability and students' well-being. *Assessment in Education: Principles, Policy & Practice* 24(1): 1–3.

Hutchings M (2015) *The impact of accountability measures on children and young people*. National Union of Teachers. Available at: https://my.chartered.college/wp-content/uploads/2021/10/Impact-of-Accountability-on-Young-People.pdf (accessed 22 November 2024).

Kluger AN and DeNisi A (1996) The effects of feedback interventions on performance: A historical review, a meta-analysis, and a preliminary feedback intervention theory. *Psychological Bulletin* 119(2): 254–284.

Lough C (2020) Dylan Wiliam: 'Immoral' to teach 'too full' curriculum. *TES*, 28 April. Available at: https://tes.com/magazine/archive/dylan-wiliam-immoral-teach-too-full-curriculum (accessed 26 November 2024).

Muijs D (2022) Motivation and learning: What comes first? In: *Education Ruminations*. Available at: https://educationruminations.com/2022/07/01/motivation-and-learning-what-comes-first (accessed 11 September 2024).

National Foundation for Education Research (NFER) (nd) *An introduction to formative and summative assessment*. Available at: https://nfer.ac.uk/assessment-hub/an-introduction-to-formative-and-summative-assessment (accessed 2 November 2024).

Oates T (2024) *The COVID-19 pandemic may be a thing of the past – its impact in schools is not*. ASCL. Available at: https://ascl.org.uk/ASCL/media/ASCL/News/Press%20releases/The-COVID-19-pandemic-may-be-a-thing-of-the-past.pdf (accessed 26 November 2024).

Schofield A (2023) Let's talk about disadvantage: The fundamental importance of oracy in closing the gap. *Impact* 19: 36–39.

Schools, Students and Teachers Network (SSAT) (nd) *Embedding formative assessment*. Available at: https://ssatuk.co.uk/cpd/teaching-and-learning/embedding-formative-assessment (accessed 4 November 2024).

The Sutton Trust (2024) *Inequality in Early Years education*. Available at: https://suttontrust.com/our-research/inequality-in-early-years-education (accessed 1 November 2024).

Wiliam D (2014) *Redesigning Schooling – 8: Principled assessment design*. SSAT. Available at: https://webcontent.ssatuk.co.uk/wp-content/uploads/2013/09/RS8-Principled-assessment-design-chapter-one.pdf (accessed 26 November 2024).

Wiliam D, Fisher D and Frey N (2024) *Student Assessment: Better Evidence, Better Decisions, Better Learning*. London: SAGE Publications.

Wiliam D and Leahy S (2014) *Sustaining formative assessment with teacher learning communities*. Learning Sciences Dylan Wiliam Center. Available at: https://commoncorediva.com/wp-content/uploads/2015/08/sustaining-tlcs-20140829.pdf (accessed 26 November 2024).

Wisniewski B, Zierer K and Hattie J (2020) The power of feedback revisited: A meta-analysis of educational feedback research. *Frontiers in Psychology* 10: 3087.

Yeager DS, Purdie-Vaughns V, Garcia J et al. (2014) Breaking the cycle of mistrust: Wise interventions to provide critical feedback across the racial divide. *Journal of Experimental Psychology: General* 143(2): 804–824.

Zhao Y (2016) *Counting What Counts: Reframing Education Outcomes.* Bloomington, IN: Solution Tree Press.

PROFESSIONAL PRINCIPLE 2

Leaders understand the characteristics of effective professional development

CHAPTER 5

Prioritising teacher growth and development

Haili Hughes, *Director of Education, IRIS Connect, UK; Principal Lecturer, University of Sunderland, UK*

This chapter will consider:
- why teacher professional development (PD) is important
- what evidence says makes for effective PD
- some of the challenges leaders should be aware of when it comes to PD
- how leaders can know whether PD is effective.

What teachers do in the classroom really matters. As the *Carter review of initial teacher training (ITT)* (2015, p. 3) states: 'No matter how well organised or detailed the curriculum, how grand or well-resourced the building, what really matters most in a child's education is the quality of the teaching.' A report by the Sutton Trust identified six key elements of effective teaching, with a strong focus on factors like subject knowledge, effective classroom management and quality of instruction (Coe et al., 2014). They concluded that improving teaching quality is the most effective way in which to raise student achievement, especially for disadvantaged students. Therefore, the professional learning of teachers should be one of the most salient priorities in a school, as it is a critical factor in improving both teacher performance and student outcomes. The benefit of well-designed PD goes beyond individual teachers. It impacts on school culture, instructional quality and overall educational equity for students. Therefore, the content, sequencing and means of delivery of teacher learning cannot be left to chance, and instead must be carefully crafted to meet the needs of colleagues at varying levels of expertise.

What does effective professional development look like?

In 2002, Joyce and Showers made significant contributions to the research on teacher PD with their work on models of professional learning and the impact of training on teacher effectiveness. Their research focused on how to ensure that PD results in sustained changes in teaching practice and improved student outcomes. They emphasised that a single session delivered by a facilitator is unlikely to result in positive changes in a teacher's classroom. Instead, sessions need to be followed by ongoing, job-embedded support through peer coaching or mentoring. The peer coaching that they described followed a cycle of observation, support and feedback, and was much more likely to bridge the gap between theory and practice, helping teachers to refine and sustain new teaching techniques. They also identified four different components of effective teacher PD:

- presentation of theory
- modelling
- practice with feedback
- coaching for application.

Sessions that missed out one or more of these components resulted in low transfer of new skills to the classroom. Joyce and Showers (2002) argued that up to 90 per cent of the transfer to classroom practice comes from ongoing coaching and feedback rather than from one-time training sessions.

The Education Endowment Foundation (EEF) (2021) built on this with their extensive research on teacher PD, which highlighted that high-quality PD has a positive impact on student outcomes, especially when it is designed to promote effective teaching practices. Helpfully, for school leaders, the report also highlighted several core elements that are essential for effective PD. These features include a focus on subject-specific content, and PD that is sustained over a period of time, with time for teachers to practise and embed new strategies in their teaching, and active learning for teachers (such as through role-playing, collaborative problem-solving and practising new strategies). As well as this, the report identified that collaboration and peer support, through coaching and mentoring, also increase the likelihood that teachers will successfully transfer new skills from PD into their teaching practice.

Poor PD is closely linked to teacher retention issues. When teachers do not receive effective, relevant and ongoing PD, it often leads to lower job satisfaction, feelings of stagnation and decreased motivation, which ultimately contribute to higher turnover rates. Effective PD provides teachers with opportunities to improve their skills, adapt to new teaching methodologies and address classroom challenges. However, when PD is lacking or poorly designed, such as being irrelevant, infrequent or generic, it fails to address these needs, leaving teachers feeling unsupported in their professional growth. According to Darling-Hammond et al. (2017), teachers who experience high-quality PD that is content-focused, collaborative and sustained over time are more likely to feel competent and stay in their roles. In contrast, when PD is inadequate, teachers are more likely to feel disengaged and consider leaving.

Mechanisms for effective professional development

Perhaps the most practical tools to come from the EEF (2021) report were the recommendations for specific mechanisms that should be included in school PD sessions and which help to influence how teachers change their classroom behaviour. These mechanisms were split into four categories:

- building knowledge
- motivating teachers
- developing teaching techniques
- embedding practice.

These mechanisms should not be a tick-box approach but should be part of a whole-school approach to professional learning, which is supported by school leadership and integrated into the school's wider improvement plans. This whole-school approach ensures that PD aligns with broader school goals and is seen as part of an ongoing process of teacher growth rather than an isolated activity. Teachers also need support to have the time, resources and encouragement needed to implement what they have learned. As well as addressing the specific needs of all teachers, rather than taking a one-size-fits-all approach, the EEF (2021) suggests that PD should be tailored to the teacher's subject area or phase and be centred around the specific challenges that they face in the classroom. These challenges, or 'wicked problems' (Rittel and Webber, 1973), exist because schools are complex environments, and practical PD that seeks to help teachers to solve some of these problems can be an effective approach for those leading PD in schools to take.

The challenges of designing and embedding effective professional development in schools

Despite the clear benefits of high-quality PD, the EEF (2021) also acknowledges several challenges to ensuring its effectiveness. Perhaps one of the biggest barriers is implementation fidelity. There is often a gap between the knowledge acquired during PD sessions and practical application in the classroom. Without sufficient support, follow-up, and prompts and cues, teachers may struggle to implement new strategies. Time constraints can also be a blocker. Many teachers also face challenges related to time and workload, which can make it difficult to engage fully with sustained PD programmes. In his book *Motivated Teaching* (2020), Peps Mccrea suggests that changing a teacher's habits can be tough because teaching involves a high cognitive load, with teachers constantly juggling multiple tasks. As a result, many actions become habitual because this reduces the cognitive burden. However, this automaticity makes it difficult to notice ineffective habits and consciously change them. Therefore, those leading PD need to think carefully about implementation and the ongoing support that they offer to teachers at different stages of their careers.

Teacher expertise

Research on teacher expertise explores how experienced and highly skilled teachers develop their knowledge, practices and decision-making capabilities over time. The literature generally focuses on the distinction between novice and expert teachers, but the 'Dreyfus model of skill acquisition' (Dreyfus and Dreyfus, 1980) describes how individuals progress through five stages of expertise. Three of these are exemplified here:

1. **Novice:** Novice teachers rely heavily on rules, procedures and external guidance. They follow prescribed teaching methods rigidly and focus on surviving day-to-day classroom challenges. At this stage, teachers do not yet have the ability to make independent decisions or adapt to unexpected situations.

2. **Advanced beginner:** Advanced beginners start to recognise patterns and develop a deeper understanding of teaching beyond basic rules. However, they still lack a broad perspective and rely on guidelines to inform their practice. At this stage, teachers can handle routine tasks but struggle with complex or novel situations. In the first five years, one in three teachers also leave the profession, just as they are beginning to master their craft. We need to provide motivation and purpose to keep these teachers going, so effective PD can establish greater levels of expertise and, with it, confidence and enjoyment of their work.

3. **Expert:** Expert teachers operate intuitively and can respond to classroom situations almost automatically, without needing to consciously think through every decision. They can improvise and adjust their teaching strategies in real time, responding to the specific needs of their students with a high level of precision. Experts have an embodied understanding of their practice, meaning that their decision-making is fluid and deeply embedded in their experience.

According to the Dreyfus model, expertise in teaching is primarily developed through experience and practice. It takes time and consistent reflection to move from rule-based behaviour to intuitive, expert-level performance. As teachers progress through the stages, they become more intuitive in their decision-making. Expert teachers can make rapid judgements and adjust to complex classroom situations fluidly, whereas novices and advanced beginners rely on guidelines and external feedback. However, the progression from novice to expert is not always linear. Teachers may oscillate between stages, depending on new challenges or changes in teaching contexts.

Dreyfus and Dreyfus's (1980) research suggests that effective PD should be differentiated according to the teacher's stage of expertise. According to Berliner (2001), expert teachers demonstrate adaptive expertise, meaning that they are flexible and can modify their teaching strategies to meet the needs of different students and situations. Unlike routine expertise, which focuses on repeated practices, adaptive expertise allows teachers to respond effectively to new challenges and diverse student needs. In a time of teacher-retention problems, this move towards adaptive expertise and PD that focuses on professional growth by taking expertise into account is also vitally important. This is because it fosters a sense of professional growth and mastery, as teachers are regularly engaging with new ideas, refining their skills and improving their practices. This ongoing learning can help to keep teachers motivated and engaged in their work. Research suggests that teachers who feel that they are improving their craft and making a positive impact on student learning are more likely to stay in the profession (Ingersoll, 2001). The opportunity for professional growth, a key feature of adaptive expertise, is linked to higher job satisfaction and lower turnover (Carver-Thomas and Darling-Hammond, 2017). Furthermore, teachers with adaptive expertise are often better equipped to handle classroom challenges because they can draw on a range of strategies and approaches. This flexibility can lead to less frustration and burnout, as teachers feel more in control and capable of addressing problems, rather than being stuck in ineffective routines. This, in turn, can reduce the likelihood of leaving the profession. So, what practical steps can leaders take to harness the expertise in their settings, and what should PD focus on?

A professional development curriculum

In their book *The CPD Curriculum: Creating Conditions for Growth*, Mark and Zoe Enser (2021) recommend that PD should be treated as a structured, coherent curriculum, with long-term goals, a clear progression and ongoing learning opportunities. Just as a student curriculum is planned to ensure deep learning over time, PD should be designed with careful planning and sequencing to help teachers to develop over the course of their careers.

One of the ways in which PD can harness the expertise in schools is through taking more of a collaborative approach to PD, where teachers work together, share expertise and learn from each other. This could take the form of professional learning communities (PLCs), peer observations or coaching. There have been some great recent examples where this approach has worked, such as the Maths Hub programme, organised by NCETM (National Centre for Excellence in the Teaching of Mathematics). They created a collaborative culture for maths teacher PD within and between schools throughout England to improve maths education for all (Boylan et al., 2018). This has been funded by the Department for Education and has made a huge difference to maths mastery in England.

There is also strong evidence that approaches such as instructional coaching can yield significant benefits for improving both teacher practice and student outcomes (Kraft and Blazar, 2018). In their paper, Kraft and Blazar define instructional coaching as a one-on-one PD model where a coach (usually an experienced teacher or education specialist) works closely with a teacher over an extended period. The coaching relationship focuses on providing targeted, personalised feedback and support to help teachers to improve specific aspects of their practice. Instructional coaching also emphasises active learning through practice, reflection and immediate feedback, which means that teachers are more likely to apply new teaching strategies when they have a coach supporting them through the implementation process.

However, there are many challenges to scaling instructional coaching across a school – perhaps the most difficult is capacity. Headteachers do not have enough resources to offer staff one-to-one coaching, which is why PLCs can be so effective. Another barrier is ensuring that coaches are well-trained, experienced educators who are skilled at both the technical aspects of teaching and providing constructive, supportive feedback. Poorly implemented coaching programmes may not yield the same positive results and, indeed, may result in a loss of teacher motivation if they are formulaic and do not take into account teacher expertise. There are also many other forms of teacher collaboration and coaching that may be just as effective. These could include action research cycles, reciprocal and group-based coaching and Lesson Study. The key is to not just decide to do instructional coaching because everybody else is doing it; leaders need to know what has the best chance of working in their context, with their teachers, to help them to solve the problems that they are facing in helping their students to achieve their best possible outcomes.

Is it working? Measuring the impact

Finally, it's important to regularly assess the effectiveness of PD programmes. The EEF recommends using multiple data sources to evaluate the impact of PD. These should include both qualitative and quantitative data to capture the full effect of PD on teacher practice and student learning.

Data sources may include:

- teacher self-assessments and reflections
- classroom observations
- student outcomes
- teacher surveys and interviews
- peer feedback.

Combining and triangulating these data sources gives a more comprehensive picture of how PD has influenced teaching and learning in the school and may inform future PD plans, as some things may need to be adapted or revisited.

Thomas Guskey's (2000) book, *Evaluating Professional Development*, is also useful, as it breaks evaluation of PD down into five different levels:

1. participants' reaction
2. participants' learning
3. organisation and support
4. participants' use of new knowledge/skills
5. student learning outcomes.

If leaders evaluate their PD using these five levels, they can help to break down what needs they are addressing and what impact they are evaluating. Guskey also points out that all levels are important and should be considered.

Measuring the impact of PD is vital, as leaders need to get this right. Teachers who believe that they are improving their practice and making a meaningful impact on student learning are more likely to stay in the profession. Any PD opportunities need to involve high levels of self-efficacy for staff. This contributes to higher job satisfaction and a stronger sense of purpose, which are crucial for retaining teachers in the profession, as well as impacting on student attainment, as they will have the most effective teachers in front of them.

> ## Questions for reflection
> - What does PD look like in your setting? To what extent does it align with the evidence around effective PD?
> - Do all those involved in designing and delivering PD understand the characteristics of effective PD?
> - How confident are you that the PD that teachers receive is effective? How do you evaluate the impact of PD (and how do you use this evaluation to continually improve your approach)?

References

Berliner DC (2001) Learning about and learning from expert teachers. *International Journal of Educational Research* 35(5): 463–482.

Boylan M, Maxwell B, Wolstenholme C et al. (2018) The mathematics teacher exchange and 'mastery' in England: The evidence for the efficacy of component practices. *Education Sciences* 8(4): 202.

Carter A (2015) *Carter review of initial teacher training (ITT)*. Department for Education. Available at: https://assets.publishing.service.gov.uk/media/5a7d63c3ed915d2d2ac08a94/Carter_Review.pdf (accessed 25 November 2024).

Carver-Thomas D and Darling-Hammond L (2017) *Teacher turnover: why it matters and what we can do about it*. Learning Policy Institute. Available at: https://learningpolicyinstitute.org/product/teacher-turnover-report (accessed 25 November 2024).

Coe R, Aloisi C, Higgins S et al. (2014) *What makes great teaching? Review of the underpinning research.* The Sutton Trust. Available at: https://suttontrust.com/researcharchive/great-teaching (accessed 25 November 2024).

Darling-Hammond L, Hyler ME and Gardner M (2017) *Effective teacher professional development.* Learning Policy Institute. Available at: https://learningpolicyinstitute.org/sites/default/files/product-files/Effective_Teacher_Professional_Development_REPORT.pdf (accessed 29 November 2024).

Dreyfus SE and Dreyfus HL (1980) *A five-stage model of the mental activities involved in directed skill acquisition.* University of California. Available at: https://apps.dtic.mil/sti/tr/pdf/ADA084551.pdf (accessed 25 November 2024).

Education Endowment Foundation (EEF) (2021) *Effective professional development: Guidance report.* Available at: https://d2tic4wvo1iusb.cloudfront.net/production/eef-guidance-reports/effective-professional-development/EEF-Effective-Professional-Development-Guidance-Report.pdf?v=1727024636 (accessed 25 November 2024).

Enser M and Enser Z (2021) *The CPD Curriculum: Creating Conditions for Growth.* Carmarthen: Crown House.

Guskey T (2000) *Evaluating Professional Development.* Thousand Oaks, CA: Corwin Press.

Ingersoll RM (2001) Teacher turnover and teacher shortages: An organizational analysis. *American Educational Research Journal* 38(3): 499–534.

Joyce BR and Showers B (2002) *Student Achievement Through Staff Development,* 3rd ed. Alexandria, VA: Association for Supervision and Curriculum Development.

Kraft MA and Blazar D (2018) The effect of teaching coaching on instruction and achievement: A meta-analysis of the causal evidence. *Review of Educational Research* 88(4): 547–588.

Mccrea P (2020) *Motivated Teaching.* North Charleston, SC: CreateSpace Independent Publishing Platform.

Rittel HWJ and Webber MM (1973) Dilemmas in a general theory of planning. *Policy Sciences* 4(2): 155–169.

PROFESSIONAL PRINCIPLE 3

Leaders have a deep understanding of their school(s), and also the wider educational context

CHAPTER 6

Evidence and context

Jess Mahdavi-Gladwell, *Deputy Head, Robson House, UK*

This chapter will consider:
- the importance of context in taking an evidence-informed approach to school leadership
- the multiple layers of context that leaders might consider
- what context-responsive leadership could look like in practice.

The use of research evidence to inform education policy and practice can support school leaders to ensure that all children benefit from the most appropriate and effective methods and pedagogies. Leaders can utilise research to ensure that teachers and support staff use their limited time in the most impactful ways possible.

It may be helpful at this point to delve a little deeper into the notion of evidence-informed practice and the importance of context when applying ideas from research into schools.

What do we mean by evidence-informed practice?

Evidence-informed practice is represented in **Figure 6.1**. This diagram conceptualises evidence-informed practice as the space that exists when context, research evidence, and teacher experience, expertise and judgement are all considered in the process of decision-making.

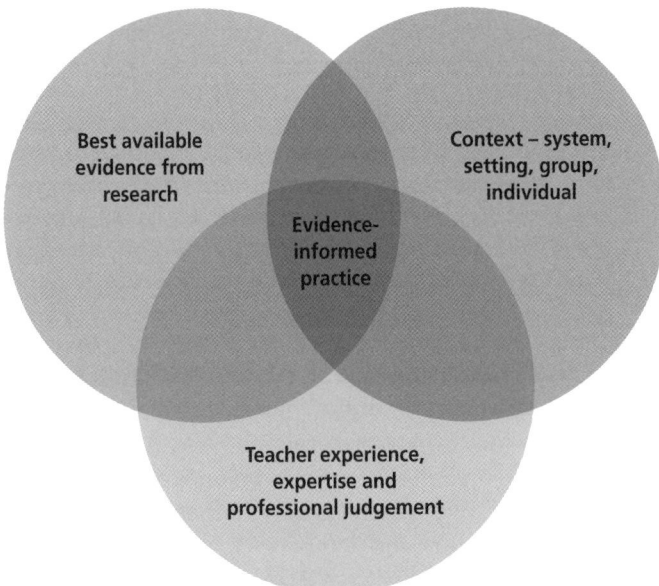

Figure 6.1: Evidence-informed practice (adapted from Scutt, 2018)

These three areas all have an impact and are all experienced differently by individuals who work in education. This chapter specifically addresses context in relation to leadership practices, while also acknowledging the crucial influence of and interaction with the other two areas.

Context: system, setting, group, individual

When considering the relevance and validity of research, the influence of context cannot be underestimated. There are a vast range of situations in which teaching and learning happen: we have primary schools with and without nursery provision, secondary schools with and without sixth-form provision; we have middle schools, grammar schools, special schools, student referral units, maintained schools, academies, independent schools and boarding schools to name but a few. There are schools of different sizes, and we also see variety in relation to ethos and values: is a school very formal or more relaxed? Teachers might be called 'Miss' or

'Madam' and 'Sir', or by their first name. Situational variety, which goes far beyond these examples, increases the importance of knowing about the specific context within which research was initially carried out. That knowledge then allows for careful reflection on the influence of that context, and the similarities and differences between that context and the context in which the research findings may be applied.

When considering a piece of research as an influencing factor for decision-making, the system, setting, group and individuals in your school will all have an impact. The remainder of this section is not intended to be an exhaustive list of actions, but gives examples of some system-level differences that could influence how information about context might impact the relevance of findings.

The education system within which a study was carried out should be included in a research report or article. Information about the context the research applies to allows you to ascertain whether the findings may be more likely to apply to an Early Years Foundation Stage (EYFS), primary or secondary setting. There might also be information about whether the schools in a study were based in inner-city, rural or coastal areas, or indeed, whether the participants were drawn from a range of schools in different geographical locations, whether the participants attended (or worked at) an independent school or a maintained school, and whether the schools sampled were mainstream, alternative provision, faith or church schools, for example.

As a school leader, you will need to consider these factors when deciding whether to implement an initiative or change a practice. In many cases, common sense tells us that something that works for typically-developing 17-year-olds is not easily transferable to a class of typically-developing five-year-olds, in that their prior learning and understanding of language and developmentally appropriate focus demands are not comparable.

Additionally, information about the participant group could include, for example, whether any or all of the participants had special educational needs and disabilities (SEND) – and perhaps which of the four areas of need outlined in the *SEND Code of practice* (DfE and DHSC, 2014) are represented in the participant group – or indeed, whether participants with SEND were excluded from the study. The reader might also be informed as to whether the participants were based in settings with mixed-age classes or whether the class size was perhaps much smaller than is typical.

Contextual information builds on other information that can be inferred from the findings shared. An approach that is shown to be effective for children in the EYFS in the UK education system would likely not show the same impact in an A-level classroom, due to students' starting points. An intervention that is found to be effective when delivered one-on-one with one child with an education, health and care plan (EHCP) for 30 minutes a day may not be possible to implement for eight children in a different setting. Data showing the effectiveness of a social-skills intervention in a mainstream classroom may not indicate that the intervention will be equally useful in a setting in which all students have significant language and communication needs.

As you read this, you may be wondering what this means for you and for your setting. My own experience in mainstream and non-mainstream settings, and in primary and secondary schools, has led to my belief that there is usually more to be found in common than that which divides us, for both educators and learners, across sectors and settings. When reading research that was carried out in a setting different from your own, there is likely to be something of use, even if it's a reason to not do something, thus saving time, energy and money. Cultivating a culture of wondering, of thinking together without fear of being 'wrong', is a good way in which to support your staff team to begin or continue their journey of using research to inform their practice. If you know and celebrate the strengths of your team, the responsibility for developing research engagement as part of your school culture can be a shared effort, where a core group can empower and encourage staff to engage with research. Leat et al. (2014) reflect on both the challenges and benefits of engaging with research. This journey is not one that is limited to curriculum subjects. Pastoral staff can also share in this drive, especially when policies – perhaps behaviour or anti-bullying – are revisited.

The replicability of findings can also inform decisions about how reliable and applicable a study is. Lykken (1968) describes different ways in which the replicability of findings can be tested, whether replication is attempted through using the same method (in the same population or a different population – sometimes called close replication), using a different method to investigate the same research question (sometimes called conceptual replication), or reanalysing previously collected datasets. In practical terms, if we test the reliability of a study looking at the impact of using an online tool to learn multiplication facts, using data collected by the online tool, then close replication could involve using the same online tool in a different class or school, conceptual replication could measure oral responses to multiplication questions, or data from maths assessments earlier in the year could be reanalysed. Three datasets could then be compared to the original findings to check for similarity.

Context and its interaction with teacher experience, expertise and professional judgement

Teacher experience, expertise and professional judgement are measured for different reasons. For example, datasets include teacher assessment in some subjects at the end of Key Stage 2; the sixth teachers' standard (DfE, 2011) states clearly that as part of their duties, teachers are expected to assess accurately and to use these teacher assessments productively, mentioning both formative and summative assessment. Further examples of recording and using professional judgement and expertise include the 'assess, plan, do and review' cycles that form the graduated approach outlined in the *SEND Code of practice* (DfE and DHSC, 2014). Additionally, teacher assessment is used when reviewing the impact of some aspects of provision set out in EHCPs. The *SEND Code of practice* (DfE and DHSC, 2014) states that the local authority must consider 'evidence of the child or young person's academic attainment (or developmental milestones in younger children) and rate of progress' (p. 144), which would usually come, at least in part, from teacher assessment. Professional judgement is also drawn upon here, with the local authority needing to consider 'evidence that where progress has been made, it has only been as the result of much additional intervention and support over and above that which is usually provided' (DfE and DHSC, 2014, p. 145), and such information would usually be compiled by the SENDCo with input from the class or subject teacher(s).

During the COVID-19 pandemic, teacher assessment was used to award teacher-assessed grades and centre-assessed grades in place of the usual public examinations for GCSE and A-level courses. Although many aspects of practice were similar in the processes involved in collecting information, Vitello and Leech (2022) also found notable variances between and within centres. This is one example where, in the midst of imperfect and unforeseen circumstances, teachers' experience and judgement in their individual contexts gave rise to a solution. This solution, though imperfect, represents teachers' best, taking into account understandable conflicts in perceptions of the importance of different aspects of 'fairness' (Crisp et al., 2024).

It is fair to assume that, in most cases, an individual's expertise and judgement will increase alongside experience, with influences from professional development also supporting them. Knowing your own phase, subject or other specialism deeply also impacts how effectively the context of a piece of research can be evaluated. It is important to consider that many studies remove 'outliers' from their data. Although this is understandable in some contexts, it means that a study that looks at the impact of introducing a new strategy to develop oracy skills might not include participants with language and communication needs, and a teacher working with those students would need to evaluate findings accordingly.

Context and school leadership

As a school leader, considerations of context are important not only when interpreting ideas from research for your setting, but in all decision-making you are tasked with, including decisions around curriculum, teacher development, school development and community engagement. Having a deep understanding of school context, local context and wider educational context will ensure that you are well positioned to make the best possible decisions for the students in your setting.

Drawing on the professional principles, **Table 6.1** below captures some of the nuance and depth of contextual knowledge that may be required when it comes to day-to-day decision-making:

Contextual knowledge required for leaders	How is this knowledge applied?
An understanding of the complex influences and range of factors that affect children and young people within their setting(s)	Informs strategic decisions about support – i.e. how to respond to these influences in order to create an inclusive and equitable learning environment
A deep understanding of the quality of teaching and learning within and across school(s), including the strengths, challenges, opportunities and priorities for improvement	Informs professional development planning, school development planning; enables recognition and sharing of effective practice and identification of support/need
An understanding of how the school can interact with the local community	Enables teachers, leaders and students to contribute and respond to the needs of the community and vice versa
An understanding of the wider education landscape and local, national and global trends in education	Enables leaders to evaluate the relevance for their own setting in order to respond appropriately
A secure knowledge of legal, and local and national frameworks; an understanding of education policy	Enables leaders to interpret requirements into practice, recognising the implications for teachers, the school and the wider profession

Table 6.1: Examples of contextual knowledge required for decision-making

LEADERSHIP INSIGHT

Context-responsive leadership

Narinder Gill, School Improvement Director, Elevate Multi Academy Trust, UK; Former Headteacher, Hunslet Moor Primary School, UK

Introduction

The case of Hunslet Moor Primary School in Beeston, Leeds, offers valuable insights into the power of context-responsive leadership in transforming educational institutions facing complex challenges (Darley and Gill, 2018). Context-responsive leadership begins with a deep understanding of the unique circumstances of a school and its community. At Hunslet Moor, this meant recognising the interplay of socio-economic challenges, political tensions and cultural diversity. Situated in a community with high levels of socio-economic deprivation, the school struggled with low academic attainment, racial divides and limited parental engagement. Tim Brighouse (2019) emphasises that effective leadership in challenging settings requires patience and contextual literacy. This principle remains crucial in today's rapidly changing educational landscape, where schools increasingly serve diverse populations and face complex societal issues.

Understanding the context

The senior leadership team at Hunslet Moor recognised that addressing external stereotypes and community mistrust would require prioritising the school's role as an anchor for shared aspirations and positive change. We began by identifying some key challenges that the school community was facing and that had to be addressed:

- low academic achievement in literacy and numeracy
- a lack of student and parental confidence in education
- limited opportunities for collaboration across ethnic groups
- an outdated curriculum ill-suited to the community's needs.

Building community engagement

While a school's boundaries may be physical, its influence and responsibility extend far beyond its gates. As Mick Waters (2018, p. 115) states, 'The vicious circle of poor performance and economic and social deprivation can only be broken permanently through sustained growth built on community and involvement linked to growing achievement and self-belief.' Recognising this, the school began to develop initiatives to bridge divides and foster collaboration.

Practical actions

1. **Faith trails and cross-cultural learning:** Hunslet Moor organised faith trails, inviting children and parents to explore local places of worship, promoting mutual understanding and respect across religious groups.

2. **Global citizenship programmes:** A project funded by the British Council connected Hunslet Moor students with peers in Botswana, encouraging them to explore shared values and cultural differences, fostering a global perspective.

3. **Community leadership meetings:** To address racial tensions, the school convened a meeting with local religious leaders and community activists. This facilitated shared understanding and collaboration despite differing perspectives.

4. **International Women's Day:** We celebrated women's achievements in an attempt to foster connections across the community so that women and girls felt empowered.

5. **Charity dinner projects:** Students formed 'companies' to plan and execute annual, themed charity dinners, integrating academic learning with entrepreneurial skills and community engagement.

Although balancing inclusivity with differing community perspectives often proved challenging, by actively involving all stakeholders, the school fostered trust and a shared vision for its students, exemplifying the assertion of Khalifa et al. (2016) that culturally responsive school leaders can cultivate trust-based relationships to counter stereotypes.

A culturally responsive curriculum

Hunslet Moor's curriculum was redesigned to address low engagement and achievement while promoting inclusivity. Previously reliant on rigid frameworks, the school shifted to a deeper shared understanding, driven by clear principles and values that were focused on tolerance, working together, community engagement and developing core English and maths skills.

Specific changes

- **Streamlining content:** The curriculum was aligned with the minimum entitlement from the national curriculum while incorporating broader goals, such as fostering teamwork and tolerance.
- **Themed weeks:** Cultural celebrations and themed projects engaged students in exploring their identities and heritage. These included projects tied to local history and global citizenship, with the goal being for students to thrive when they see their cultural identities mirrored in their learning experiences, thereby fostering greater engagement, as Sharma (2023) describes.

These changes not only improved academic outcomes but also bolstered students' self-confidence, parental involvement and cross-cultural tolerance.

Strengthening family engagement

Recognising the vital role of families, the school launched a 'Family Focus' programme. This six-week course, tailored to parents with English as an additional language, provided tools to support their children's learning, while also building parenting confidence. Topics included celebrating progress, understanding behaviour and fostering emotional connections. Multilingual resources, including ones that helped teaching assistants support translation, were key to overcoming language barriers, and the sessions encouraged open dialogue and mutual support among parents.

Challenging bias and promoting resilience

The leadership at Hunslet Moor championed a 'lens of potential' through which to view the community, reframing challenges as opportunities for growth. Khalifa (2016) highlights the importance of challenging deficit-based views, and Hunslet Moor's leadership team exemplified this by communicating our 'lens of potential' approach consistently through staff training, professional development and school-wide initiatives. Practical steps included:

- **staff reflection sessions:** regular meetings to explore how students' strengths could be nurtured
- **inclusive language:** reframing communications to highlight achievements and celebrate diversity
- **community conversations:** involving parents and local leaders in discussions about shared aspirations.

Balancing accountability and inclusivity

At times, maintaining high expectations while fostering a supportive environment posed a significant challenge. The leadership addressed this through:

- **weekly reviews:** leadership meetings to evaluate the balance between academic rigour and social-emotional support
- **data-driven decisions:** tracking progress in both academic skills and broader goals like collaboration and tolerance
- **feedback loops:** regular input from staff and students to ensure that strategies were effective and equitable.

Conclusion

The transformation of Hunslet Moor Primary School demonstrates the power of context-responsive leadership in addressing complex challenges. By cultivating community trust, reforming the curriculum and celebrating diversity, the school not only improved academic outcomes but also became a beacon of hope and resilience. For leaders facing similar contexts, this case study demonstrates the importance of understanding, adapting and engaging deeply with their communities to drive sustainable change.

> ## Questions for reflection
> - How well do you know and understand your school community, including the strengths and needs of students and teachers? How do you maintain and build this understanding over time in order to respond to changes?
> - Do you have a similar depth of understanding relating to the strengths and needs of your wider local community?
> - How do you ensure you keep up to date with legal frameworks, and local and national policy? Have you got a good understanding of any potential upcoming developments that you may need to be aware of?

References

Brighouse T (2019) *The English schooling system – yesterday, today but especially tomorrow: A Baker's dozen of essential changes towards a fairer deal for everyone.* The Priestley Lecture, Birmingham University, June 2019. Oxford School of Thought. Available at: https://oxfordschoolofthought.org/blog/strongthe-english-schooling-system-yesterday-today-but-especially-tomorrowstrong (accessed 6 December 2024).

Crisp V, Elliott G, Walland E et al. (2024) A structured discussion of the fairness of GCSE and A level grades in England in summer 2020 and 2021. *Research Papers in Education.* DOI: 10.1080/02671522.2024.2318046.

Darley H and Gill N (2018) *Creating Change in Urban Settings.* Norwich: Singular Publishing.

Department for Education (DfE) (2011) *Teachers' standards.* Available at: https://gov.uk/government/publications/teachers-standards (accessed 16 November 2024).

Department for Education (DfE) and Department of Health and Social Care (DHSC) (2014) *Special educational needs and disability code of practice: 0–25 years.* Available at: https://gov.uk/government/publications/send-code-of-practice-0-to-25 (accessed 16 November 2024).

Khalifa MA, Gooden MA and Davis JE (2016) Culturally responsive school leadership: A synthesis of the literature. *Review of Educational Research* 86(4): 1272–1311.

Leat D, Lofthouse R and Reid A (2014) Teachers' views: Perspectives on research engagement. *Research and teacher education: The BERA-RSA inquiry.* Newcastle University. Available at: https://ncl.ac.uk/mediav8/centre-for-learning-and-teaching/files/BERA-Paper-7-Teachers-Views-Perspectives-on-research-engagement.pdf (accessed 10 December 2024).

Lykken D (1968) Statistical significance in psychological research. *Psychological Bulletin* 70(3): 151–159.

Scutt C (2018) Is engaging with and in research a worthwhile investment for teachers? In: Carden C (ed) *Primary Teaching: Learning and Teaching in Primary Schools Today*. London: SAGE, pp. 595–610.

Sharma L (2023) *Building Culture: A Handbook to Harnessing Human Nature to Create Strong School Teams*. London: Hodder Education.

Vitello S and Leech T (2022) *What do we know about the evidence sources teachers used to determine 2021 teacher assessed grades?* Cambridge University Press & Assessment. Available at: https://files.eric.ed.gov/fulltext/ED626053.pdf (accessed 8 December 2024).

Waters M (2018) Afterword. In: Darley H and Gill N (eds) *Creating Change in Urban Settings*. Norwich: Singular Publishing, pp. 113–116.

SECTION 2 – PART 1
Professional practice: Leading school development

PROFESSIONAL PRINCIPLE 4

Leaders have a clear vision focused on achieving ambitious outcomes for all learners

CHAPTER 7

Establishing your vision

Lekha Sharma, *School Improvement Lead – Curriculum and Assessment, Avanti Schools Trust, UK*

This chapter will consider:
- what we mean when we talk about vision and why it is important
- how goal-setting or school-development activity can contribute to achieving a vision
- how leaders create buy-in, establish a sense of shared purpose and ensure alignment with organisational vision and goals.

In 2022, Coe et al. produced a model for school environment and leadership, detailing the current best bets that might guide the work of school leaders, drawing on a comprehensive review of the existing literature. This review was a promising step forward for school leaders in an otherwise sparse terrain of robust educational leadership research. The model sets out school-level factors for which there is good evidence that they support student outcomes. One of these school-level factors relates to an 'improvement mindset': the 'drive to be better' and the 'belief that better is possible' (Coe et al., 2022).

An important part of your role as an educational leader is thinking in the realm of possibility and aspiring for more and better for the students you serve. This is necessary for progress in any school but is also of crucial importance when addressing wider societal challenges, including closing the attainment gap for our most vulnerable students. Having a clear, well-articulated and context-considerate vision is one way in which leaders can cement their 'drive to be better' and offer colleagues a clear direction of travel towards growth.

What is a vision?

'For the school leader, the vision is a relatively clear, comprehensive picture of your school in the future and the goals you aspire to accomplish.' (Tomlinson, 2004, p. 144) A school vision allows you as a leader to form a clear path between the existing state of play and your ideal future state of being. It outlines a collective aspiration to colleagues, which they will form a crucial part in fulfilling. A compelling vision can provide multiple benefits for a school team. It:

- enables teams to have clarity about where the school is and where it's going next
- acts as an anchor during challenging times
- offers clear benchmarks for success
- establishes a sense of belonging.

For these reasons, it might be helpful for you to consider deeply what the vision is for your school and invest significant time in crafting the vision, ahead of sharing it with your team.

How do we create a vision?

A useful starting point for considering your vision is a question that can be posed to all leaders, whether for a school, department or particular area of responsibility: What's the dream? In an ideal world, with no barriers, what's the best-case scenario for your area of responsibility? What does that state look and feel like for your area? How are people relating and behaving in that state? How would students be impacted differently if that dream were to be realised? These questions offer a reflective opportunity for you to consider your vision and to begin to craft the language that will best capture and distil it. But for a vision to be a catalyst for sustained school improvement, it needs to be rooted in the authentic needs and demands of your context, meaning that you will need to engage in meaningful and deep sensemaking before crafting your vision.

Ancona (2011, in Snook et al., 2011) suggests the following steps that may support leaders to structure and guide their sensemaking:

1. Explore the wider system, working with others to observe what's going on – e.g. seeking out as many data sources as possible.
2. Involve others as you try to make sense of a situation.
3. Move beyond stereotypes and simplifications.
4. Learn from those closest to the front line.
5. Do not simply overlay your own existing framework of understanding onto this new situation.
6. Use images, metaphors and stories to capture the existing situation.
7. Learn from small experiments before broadening into widespread action.
8. Be aware of how your own behaviour is shaping the environment in which you work.

Barriers to sensemaking include:

1. Rigidity: Threat and fear lead to rigidity and often protect the status quo, resulting in inertia.
2. Erratic behaviour: In a panicked state, leaders may frantically search for a solution.

Particularly if you are new to a school, engaging in structured and robust sensemaking can enable you to consider what is essential for your vision and how this vision would serve the needs of the school. For example, by exploring 'the wider system' or engaging in conversations with the broader school community (e.g. parents and local members of the community), a leader will be able to enrich their understanding of what 'value points' are high priority for the school's development journey.

Engaging with different groups of stakeholders to create a vision (e.g. staff at all levels, parents, governors and students) enables a leader to refine these value points, identify a vision that captures what these different groups value and bake this into broader sensemaking around the needs of the school. In addition to this, the process may also bring to light any niche and bespoke areas that may inform the vision.

How do we articulate a vision?

In his work on communication, Fernando Flores (2013) emphasises the role that language can play in shaping and changing realities – how the words we use in the present can affect the future. The language that we use in our vision statement and the language that we use to share our vision, therefore, is critical in declaring with utter clarity and unapologetic aspiration the destination at which we hope to arrive as an organisation.

It is important to differentiate between the vision statement itself and the body of work required to disseminate, explain, embed and 'live into' the vision statement. Beginning with the language for your vision statement, it is likely to be compelling if it:

- implies a sense of collective endeavour (use of 'we' and 'together')
- is pithy and can easily be recalled
- captures the values that are held dear by the school in some way and shows how they are linked to the future direction of travel
- uses simple and clear language
- is aspirational by nature.

Take this example of a vision statement from Reach Academy Feltham, which beautifully fulfils the above criteria:

> 'The school's vision is that every single pupil will leave us with the skills, attributes and academic qualifications to go on to enjoy lives of choice and opportunity.'

Articulating the vision into a statement of some kind is one thing; sharing the vision with your team, so that they fully understand what is meant by it, why it exists in its current form and what will be done to achieve it, is another. This requires a significant investment of time and cannot be limited to training days. To truly embody the vision, colleagues need to hold it front and centre in all that they do, and this requires an ongoing emphasis on the improvement journey of the school towards that vision.

Encouraging ongoing conversation about the students that the school serves and the community context can help teams to understand the school's purpose, which likely underpins the vision, and to get to grips with the 'why'. If, for example, a school's vision is rooted in its aspiration to 'ensure that all pupils succeed so that they can go on to thrive personally and professionally', it would make sense for school improvement efforts to be focused on securing academic attainment and personal development. It is essential to embed this golden thread of understanding between the school's purpose, where it is currently and where it's going next (guided by the vision), in order for teams to truly own and drive the vision forward. It therefore stands to reason that regular conversations about the progress made towards realising that vision can also be useful ways in which to ensure that the vision is well understood and to maintain the momentum required to meet the school's aspirations.

Leaders at all levels are responsible for maintaining the focus on the school's vision, and so it is useful to work with all school leaders to keep the vision in mind when leading on their particular area. This will ensure a coordinated and strategic approach to school improvement. Leader-specific training on developing and embedding a shared language around the vision or ensuring alignment between the vision and the improvement efforts linked to their areas can strengthen a school's ability to move closer to fulfilling their vision.

How do we 'live into' our vision?

The most important part of a vision is, arguably, 'living into' the vision. By this, we mean that every colleague within a school team is able to actively play a part in realising the school's vision, albeit in different ways. Living into the vision, however, is also very challenging. The competing demands with which a school is faced on a daily basis can often drown out the more strategic and long-term focus. It is therefore essential that leaders focus conversations around living into the vision and working towards the markers of success that will enable this. In *Student-Centered Leadership*, Viviane Robinson (2011) writes that 'the more leaders focus their relationships, their work, and their learning on the core business of teaching and learning, the greater will be their focus on student outcomes' (p. 15). The skill, therefore, of discerning what contributes to or detracts from your goal, is key in safeguarding your vision so that it is not only declared and shared but also accomplished. This skill set might include:

- leaders being selective about the improvement efforts that they lead and ensuring that these are tightly linked to the genuine needs of the school and their area
- leaders having the ability to say 'no' to things, to ensure a sharp focus on making progress
- de-implementation where necessary
- leaders having ongoing conversations to moderate their own judgements of how the school is doing in relation to the vision, so that there are reliable progress markers.

Living into your vision as a leader also produces another incredibly powerful by-product. It establishes trust. Trust can be understood as the 'willingness to be vulnerable to another party based on the confidence that the latter party is (a) benevolent, (b) reliable, (c) competent, (d) honest, and (e) open.' (Tschannen-Moran and Hoy, 2000, p. 556) Therefore, by living into your vision and values, you can further establish and enhance trust with your colleagues by 'making good' on your promises and agreed ways of being. This, in turn, can positively impact school improvement, as demonstrated by Bryk and Schneider (2002, cited in Robinson, 2017), who found a causal relationship between the degree of trust among members of a school team and the degree of improvement in school outcomes.

Your vision as a leader can be incredibly potent: it can unite, motivate and inspire your staff. With a contextually appropriate vision, considered communication and a sharp focus on what matters, you are likely to move closer towards your goals at pace and, ultimately, more positively impact the students you serve.

> **Questions for reflection**
> - How might you practically make sense of your context so that you can best create a context-considerate vision?
> - How might you articulate your vision with different stakeholders so that there is a common understanding of what the vision means?
> - What practical structures, systems or habits might enable you to 'live into' your vision? How can you make the vision something that is commonly spoken about around your school?

References

Coe R, Kime S and Singleton D (2022) *A model for school environment and leadership. School environment and leadership: Evidence review*. Evidence Based Education. Available at: https://evidencebased.education/school-environment-and-leadership-evidence-review (accessed 6 November 2024).

Flores F (2013) *Conversations for Action and Collected Essays: Instilling a Culture of Commitment in Working Relationships*. North Charleston, SC: CreateSpace Independent Publishing Platform.

Robinson V (2011) *Student-Centered Leadership*. San Francisco, CA: Jossey-Bass.

Robinson V (2017) Capabilities required for leading improvement. *ACER Research Depository*. Available at: https://research.acer.edu.au/cgi/viewcontent.cgi?article=1306&context=research_conference (accessed 6 November 2024).

Snook SA, Nohria N and Khurana R (2011) *The Handbook for Teaching Leadership: Knowing, Doing, and Being*. Thousand Oaks, CA: SAGE Publications.

Tomlinson H (2004) *Educational Leadership: Personal Growth for Professional Development*. London: SAGE Publications.

Tschannen-Moran M and Hoy WK (2000) A multidisciplinary analysis of the nature, meaning, and measurement of trust. *Review of Educational Research* 70(4): 547–593.

PROFESSIONAL PRINCIPLE 5

Take an evidence-informed approach to school development

CHAPTER 8

Evidence-informed school development

Kathryn Morgan, *Senior Capacity Improvement Advisor, Teaching School Hubs Council, UK*

This chapter will consider:
- the role of research and evidence throughout the school development process (including evidence gathered from the school, and sensemaking from teachers and leaders)
- implementation and de-implementation
- managing change and getting buy-in.

'Don't design the future until you deeply understand the present.'
(Robinson, 2019)

Over the past decade, the English education system's focus on research and evidence-based resources has surged. Yet as the Education Endowment Foundation's (EEF) *A School's Guide to Implementation* (Sharples et al., 2024) notes, awareness of evidence alone doesn't guarantee improved student outcomes. Often, it's not just poor implementation but the choice of ineffective interventions (referred to as change initiatives in this chapter) that limits progress.

This chapter highlights that meaningful, sustainable improvement begins with a deep understanding of the present before designing future solutions. It explores five key elements of evidence-informed school development:

- the complexity of leading school improvement
- making evidence-informed decisions
- moving from change to improvement
- interrogating needs through theories of action and sensemaking
- the symbiotic nature of implementation and de-implementation.

Throughout this chapter, you will find opportunities to pause and reflect on each concept, applying it to your own context. Before moving on from this introduction, take a moment to consider your experience with leading change initiatives so far: What strategies or approaches have proven successful, and what challenges have emerged along the way? Reflecting on these experiences will deepen your understanding of the principles in this chapter, providing a foundation for more intentional, evidence-informed school development.

The complexity of leading school improvement

Schools are inherently complex environments, creating competing pressures on leaders' time, thinking and resources. This complexity stems from high levels of interaction between individuals and systems (Hawkins and James, 2018) and significant variation in these interactions, making cause and effect difficult to establish. Teachers and students vary in knowledge, needs, beliefs and motivations, creating a highly interactive and relatively unpredictable school environment, where it is challenging to determine which intervention will be effective and when (Kirschner and Surma, 2020). This social complexity underscores the challenges of leading school improvement (Koh and Askell-Williams, 2021).

Developing high-quality teaching within this environment is, therefore, also complex. School leaders must establish organisational conditions that support ongoing teacher development and high-quality teaching (Leithwood et al., 2019). The range of responsibilities – reflected in the 10 curriculum domains of the Department for Education's National Professional Qualifications (NPQ) frameworks – requires extensive knowledge and adds to the demands on leaders (Gilbride et al., 2023).

Such a wide set of responsibilities in a complex environment can make for an extremely demanding work brief. While school development often involves problem-solving, an overemphasis on quick solutions can lead to fragmented initiatives that dilute focus. Leaders may feel drawn to adopt popular practices from other schools or consultants, but meaningful, sustainable change requires a more focused approach. By prioritising a careful selection of evidence-informed initiatives and embedding these deeply, leaders can drive more impactful and lasting improvements.

Reflection

- What evidence do you have that each initiative you're working on is progressing meaningfully, or is your attention spread too thinly across multiple areas?
- How often do you see your team struggling with time, resources and energy due to competing priorities?
- What might this indicate about the feasibility of your current goals?

Making evidence-informed decisions

Effective implementation is key to translating research into practical changes that improve student outcomes. According to Sharples et al. (2024), effective implementation is described as 'making, and acting on, evidence-informed decisions' (p. 2) to foster sustainable improvements tailored to the school's specific needs. Schools are rich in data – visible metrics such as test scores and attendance, and less tangible insights such as student wellbeing and staff morale. This diverse information ranges in reliability, from verified records to anecdotal feedback, making decision-making complex and open to interpretation and bias. Evidence that appears effective in one classroom may not apply elsewhere (Kirschner and Surma, 2020).

Evidence-informed practice offers a deeper understanding of school needs, allowing leaders to identify where changes are most necessary. Rather than relying solely on research data, it is essential to consider various information sources, including standardised test scores, attendance and behaviour records, feedback from students and parents, teacher observations, and community needs assessments. Contextual factors, such as language diversity and socioeconomic challenges, are also vital. By blending evidence with contextual knowledge, experience and professional judgement, leaders build a strong foundation for prioritising school development (see **Figure 8.1**).

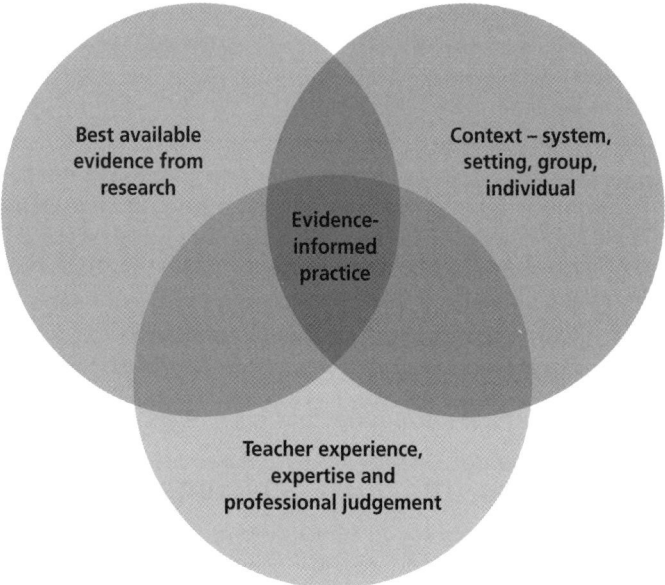

Figure 8.1: Evidence-informed practice (adapted from Scutt, 2018)

Regardless of how well supported a change initiative is, its success ultimately depends on how it influences daily staff behaviours (Sharples et al., 2024). This requires open, reflective dialogue with those involved to ensure that changes are relevant to existing practices and aligned with improvement goals.

From change to improvement

School leadership is both rewarding and challenging, driven by the commitment to uphold the highest educational standards. At its best, school change is led by leaders focused on positive impacts for students and fostering motivation and job satisfaction for staff. However, the education system's high-stakes accountability can drive an ongoing cycle of change. Over the past five years, your school may have introduced multiple initiatives, such as:

- a new curriculum and planning approach
- an instructional model for teaching and learning
- an approach to assessment
- an instructional coaching model
- a model for behaviour and inclusion
- a professional development strategy
- initiatives for attendance and parental engagement.

These examples likely understate the total changes, as they don't cover subject-specific adjustments, individual teacher development or frequent system-wide mandates. For many teachers, this volume of change can lead to reduced job satisfaction (Sikora et al., 2004) and 'change fatigue' (Bernerth et al., 2011). By dedicating time to understanding each problem, the rationale behind proposed initiatives and likely teacher responses, leaders can foster more effective, accountable improvement (Robinson, 2017). This approach includes exploring theories of action and shared sensemaking, recognising the complex interplay between individuals and systems.

> ## Questions for reflection
> - Reflecting on the list above, what recent change initiatives have taken place in your school, and are there any additional initiatives unique to your school's context and development journey?
> - What unintended consequences, if any, have emerged from these changes in terms of staff motivation, energy and retention? How might these insights shape your approach to future initiatives?

Interrogating need(s): Theories of action and sensemaking

Allocating time to examine practices underlying identified issues is essential for evidence-informed improvement. This process explores both the *proposed* theory of action (desired change) and the *existing* theory that informs current practices. According to Argyris and Schön (1996), a theory of action reveals the underlying reasons for practices through three components:

- values and beliefs driving actions
- the actions themselves
- intended and unintended consequences.

The 'engagement approach' provides a structured pathway for this investigation, building collective understanding through four steps (Robinson, 2017):

1. Define the problem.
2. Uncover tacit beliefs, values and cultural norms supporting current practices.
3. Compare the merits of current (teachers') and proposed (leaders') theories to create a shared action plan.
4. Implement and monitor the new theory of action.

This structured dialogue enhances alignment between staff practices and proposed changes, creating a collaborative, reflective environment where both existing needs and new goals are acknowledged and understood. Notably, the engagement approach also significantly supports the implementation process, ensuring that changes are embedded thoughtfully and effectively.

Sensemaking as collective action

In complex settings like schools, sensemaking is essential for navigating grey areas, where straightforward solutions are often lacking. As Holt and Cornelissen (2014) note, collective sensemaking allows leaders and staff to interpret and adapt to intricate challenges, fostering shared understanding and practical responsiveness. This approach requires flexibility rather than fixed outcomes, as seen when addressing nuanced issues like student absenteeism (Biddulph and Gilbride, 2024).

Robinson's engagement approach (2017) aids sensemaking by creating a safe holding environment (Heifetz et al., 2009), such as regular open staff forums where staff can share honest concerns and feedback. In a holding environment, leaders balance stability with enough constructive tension to encourage individuals to engage thoughtfully with change. This openness reduces the risks of imposed change, fostering trust and adaptability, as staff feel supported yet challenged to grow. By providing this space, leaders enable meaningful, sustainable development through co-construction and continuous dialogue, helping individuals to gradually adjust to new ways of thinking and working, while ensuring the collective ownership of change initiatives.

Sensemaking in practice: implementing a new behaviour policy

One school facing behaviour issues implemented a structured behaviour policy through a sensemaking process that engaged all stakeholders in building shared understanding:

- **Collaborative understanding:** Staff focus groups were held to align the policy with classroom realities, adapting it to balance consistency with practical demands.
- **Adaptive culture through feedback:** Student and parent forums gathered perspectives, fostering transparency and reinforcing behaviour expectations.
- **Safe holding environment:** Bi-weekly check-ins and termly workshops enabled ongoing adaptation, allowing staff to raise concerns and make adjustments without fear.

By embedding co-construction, adaptability and a supportive environment, this sensemaking approach fostered alignment, resilience and shared ownership. Leaders and stakeholders worked together to co-create, adapt and sustain meaningful change, transforming school behaviour culture in a complex environment.

The symbiotic nature of implementation and de-implementation

Effective implementation is crucial for meaningful, sustainable change in schools. By approaching implementation as an ongoing, collaborative process, leaders can engage stakeholders to co-create, adapt and embed initiatives that reflect the school's unique needs and culture (Sharples et al., 2024). This aligns with sensemaking, where shared understanding is built through stakeholder involvement (Robinson,

2017; Holt and Cornelissen, 2014). The EEF's *A School's Guide to Implementation* (Sharples et al., 2024) presents three principles that closely align with Robinson's (2017) engagement approach:

1. **Adopt behaviours that drive implementation:** Engaging staff to co-construct goals fosters ownership. The engagement approach (Robinson, 2017) uses structured dialogue, allowing staff to help define issues and shape strategies. In the behaviour policy case study, focus groups gave staff space to address concerns, aligning the policy with classroom realities and cultivating shared ownership.

2. **Attend to contextual factors:** Recognising each school's unique context is essential for effective, evidence-informed initiatives. The engagement approach encourages diverse community perspectives, as seen in the behaviour policy case, where student and parent forums reinforced transparency. Open dialogue and Q&A sessions fostered collaboration, making the policy more relevant and gaining community support.

3. **Use a structured, flexible process:** Implementation benefits from a structured yet adaptable process – explore, prepare, deliver and sustain. The engagement approach incorporates continuous feedback and a 'safe holding environment' for real-time adjustments. For example, bi-weekly check-ins and workshops offered staff a space to discuss and refine the policy, allowing it to adapt to classroom needs.

Together, the engagement approach (Robinson, 2017) and the EEF's principles (Sharples et al., 2024) offer a cohesive framework for embedding change. By integrating these methods, leaders can foster resilient, evidence-informed improvements that adapt meaningfully to the complexities of the school environment.

Alongside effective implementation, schools must recognise when certain practices no longer serve their purpose. De-implementation allows leaders to free up time and resources, focusing on high-impact initiatives. As Wiliam (2018) suggests, leadership often involves helping staff to prioritise 'great' practices over 'good' ones.

Mccrea (2024) describes de-implementation in three phases:

1. **Identify:** Evidence-based decisions help to identify practices that may no longer meet the school's needs or align with priorities. In the behaviour policy case, any prior practices that conflicted with the new expectations were reviewed and adjusted.
2. **Design:** Leaders can reduce, replace or rework outdated practices, enabling clearer alignment with new priorities (Hamilton et al., 2023).
3. **Implement:** The same collaborative approach used in implementation supports successful de-implementation, helping staff to navigate transitions smoothly.

In both implementing and de-implementing initiatives, evidence-informed school development involves deeply understanding the school's context, engaging in structured dialogue and nurturing conditions for change to take root. By balancing these elements, school leaders can lead sustainable improvement that is responsive to the school's unique and evolving needs.

Now you understand the present, look to the future

Now that you understand the present, you are equipped to design a meaningful and sustainable future. Evidence-informed school development requires balancing the complexities of your school environment with high-impact, well-chosen initiatives, and knowing when to implement or de-implement based on both evidence and the experiences within your community. Through collaborative sensemaking and adaptive practices, leaders can navigate the ambiguities of improvement, fostering change that is purposeful and lasting.

In a high-stakes system, the goal is not to manage change for its own sake but to ensure that it aligns deeply with your school's values and priorities. Leaders who focus on fewer, higher-impact initiatives and cultivate a reflective culture create a school environment that genuinely supports student outcomes and builds a resilient community.

> **Questions for reflection**
> - What steps can you take to engage staff, students and parents in the implementation or removal of initiatives, ensuring that their perspectives shape the process in ways that improve day-to-day practice?
> - Which current practices or initiatives might be taking time or resources away from your core goals, and how can you create supportive forums (e.g. staff workshops or feedback sessions) to help staff to adapt to necessary changes?
> - How will you design the future of your school in a way that truly enables the implementation of meaningful change initiatives to meet the evolving needs of your students and school community?

References

Argyris C and Schön D (1996) *Organizational Learning II: Theory, Method and Practice*. Reading, MA: Addison-Wesley.

Bernerth JB, Walker HJ and Harris SG (2011) Change fatigue development and initial validation of a new measure. *Work and Stress Journal* 25(4): 321–337.

Biddulph J and Gilbride N (2024) Playful school leadership: Being serious about leadership playfully. In: Durning A, Baker S and Ramchandani P (eds) *Empowering Play in Primary Education*. London: Routledge, pp. 147–166.

Gilbride N, James C and Carr S (2023) The ways school headteachers/principals in England at different stages of adult ego development work with organisational complexity. *Educational Management Administration and Leadership*. Online: DOI: 17411432231170581.

Hamilton A, Hattie J and Wiliam D (2023) *Making Room for Impact: A De-Implementation Guide for Educators*. Thousand Oaks, CA: Corwin Press.

Hawkins M and James C (2018) Developing a perspective on schools as complex, evolving, loosely linking systems. *Educational Management Administration and Leadership* 46(5): 729–748.

Heifetz R, Grashow A and Linsky M (2009) *The Practice of Adaptive Leadership: Tools and Tactics for Changing Your Organization and the World*. Boston, MA: Harvard Business Press.

Holt R and Cornelissen J (2014) Sensemaking revisited. *Management Learning Journal* 45(3): 525–553.

Kirschner P and Surma T (2020) Developing evidence-informed teaching techniques to support effective learning. *Impact* Issue 10.

Koh GA and Askell-Williams H (2021) Sustainable school improvement in complex adaptive systems: A scoping review. *Review of Education* 9(1): 281–314.

Leithwood K, Harris A and Hopkins D (2019) Seven strong claims about successful school leadership revisited. *School Leadership and Management* 40(4): 1–18.

Mccrea P (2024) De-implementation. In: *Evidence Snacks*. Available at: https://snacks.pepsmccrea.com/p/de-implementation (accessed 31 August 2024).

Robinson VMJ (2017) *Reduce Change to Increase Improvement*. Thousand Oaks, CA: Corwin Press.

Robinson VMJ (2019) Reduce change to increase improvement. In: *World Visible Learning Conference*, Edinburgh, UK, March 2019.

Scutt C (2018) Is engaging with and in research a worthwhile investment for teachers? In: Carden C (ed) *Primary Teaching: Learning and Teaching in Primary Schools Today*. London: SAGE, pp. 595–610.

Sharples J, Eaton J and Boughelaf J (2024) *A School's Guide to Implementation*. Education Endowment Foundation. Available at: https://educationendowmentfoundation.org.uk/education-evidence/guidance-reports/implementation (accessed 8 November 2024).

Sikora P, Beaty E and Forward J (2004) Updating theory on organizational stress: The synchronous multiple overlapping change (AMOC) model of workplace stress. *Human Resource Development Review* 3(1): 3–35.

Wiliam D (2018) Tweet, 13 November 2018. Available at: https://x.com/dylanwiliam/status/1062144139993776128 (accessed 31 August 2024).

PROFESSIONAL PRINCIPLE 6

Engage in critical evaluation and reflection to inform strategic choices

CHAPTER 9

Strategic evaluation for school leadership

Owen Carter, *Co-Founder and Director, ImpactEd Group, UK*

This chapter will consider:
- strategic, evidence-informed evaluation at the heart of school development and decision-making
- the value of inquiry – asking questions, gathering and triangulating useful data and evidence, and seeking input from others
- how leaders might avoid making assumptions and be aware of how their biases can influence their interpretation or decision-making.

In our schools, we want to do what works. Money is restricted, energy is limited and teachers' time is perhaps the most precious resource of all.

It's quite right, then, that there has been an explosion of interest in evidence-informed practice. The Education Endowment Foundation's 'Teaching and learning toolkit' (2018) – a summary of the evidence base behind different classroom practices – has been used by 70 per cent of school leaders, up from 11 per cent in 2012 (EEF, 2023).

But translating research into meaningful improvements in student outcomes is not so straightforward. Education research often shows that even the most well-designed educational interventions can have neutral or even negative effects: replicating proven approaches to impact on learning is easier said than done. Approaches that worked in one setting often do not scale in others (Durlak and DuPre, 2008).

Teachers and school leaders make hundreds of decisions each day on what to do and what not to do – from the questioning strategies that they employ, to the curriculum-design decisions that they take, through to the professional development that they provide. And so, there is a constant scale to balance. How much should those decisions be informed by external research evidence? And how much should they be informed by an understanding of local context?

This chapter argues that effective school-based evaluation is a key part of the solution. Intelligent evaluation helps leaders to assess the evidence of how initiatives are being applied in their school setting – to make them more effective, more quickly.

The chapter also provides some tools for how you can approach evaluation in your setting. In turn, we'll consider:

- what evaluation can and can't do for school decision-making
- how to approach an evaluation enquiry
- how to gather and interpret the data that you collect.

The role of evaluation in evidence-informed leadership

When we are talking about evaluation, what we're referring to is the process of assessing whether a change that was made has had the intended impact. That could be a small shift in classroom practice all the way through to a complete overhaul of school policy. Impact could refer to factors as varied as attainment outcomes, student wellbeing or destinations data. What is most important in arriving at an effective evaluation is a good understanding of the change that you are intending to make and what success would look like as a result.

This matters because implementation matters. We know, for example, that effective feedback is associated with improved learning outcomes. Yet one of the most comprehensive meta-analyses on feedback found that over a third of feedback interventions actually harmed performance (Kluger and DeNisi, 1996). As a school leader, you need to not only have confidence that the initiatives that you are prioritising are based on the evidence, but also be equipped to evaluate them locally.

Good evaluation helps to do a few things. It can:

- assess the impact of a pilot before deciding on further roll-out – for example, running an evaluation of a targeted mentoring programme in five schools, using that data to inform how the programme should be implemented before growing it across a trust
- ensure that resources are being used in the best way – such as carefully monitoring the usage of pupil premium[1] spend to ensure that it is achieving its desired impact
- inform the implementation of an approach in real time – for example, assessing whether a professional development programme for teachers is leading to changes in classroom practice and, ultimately, student outcomes.

When evaluation is done well, it can help schools to work smarter and not harder, helping them to stop doing things that are less effective and emphasise those that are more effective. Done badly, it can provide misleading data or a focus on accountability over improvement.

So, what are the common features of schools that approach evaluation well?

Designing an evaluation inquiry

A good place to start is by asking questions. Before starting any change process, a teacher or school leader could ask themselves the following prompts:

1. What is the problem that I am trying to address?

2. What is a change that I could make to address that problem?

3. How will I know if I have been successful in that change?

Let's unpack these in turn.

---

1   Additional funding for publicly funded schools in England to raise the attainment of disadvantaged pupils of all abilities.

Defining the problem

A challenge that we often face in schools is defining root causes. In the eagerness to put solutions in place, we sometimes don't spend enough time gaining a deep understanding of the challenge that we are looking to address. This can lead to investing resources in the wrong place, so that even the best-evidenced interventions don't end up sticking.

For example, at ImpactEd, we have run a large-scale national research project on improving students' attendance at school (ImpactEd, 2024). There are different levels of depth with which the attendance challenge could be defined.

At the simplest end, a school leader could start with 'attendance at our school is three percentage points below the national average'. But this doesn't tell you *why* attendance might be low or which groups are contributing to lower attendance.

You could then go one level deeper. For example, you might note that low attendance is driven predominantly by persistent absentees (those with below 90 per cent attendance) rather than severe absentees (with below 50 per cent attendance). You could expand this by looking at groups – for example, is this driven by female students in Key Stage 3?

Finally, you could go one level deeper still. You might survey young people and their families to find out what factors prevent them from attending school. These could be issues with public transport or more deeply rooted issues to do with engagement in education. Understanding those factors would then help you to be much more precise around what initiatives might help to address that challenge. An example of using these levels of depth to define a problem can be seen in **Figure 9.1**.

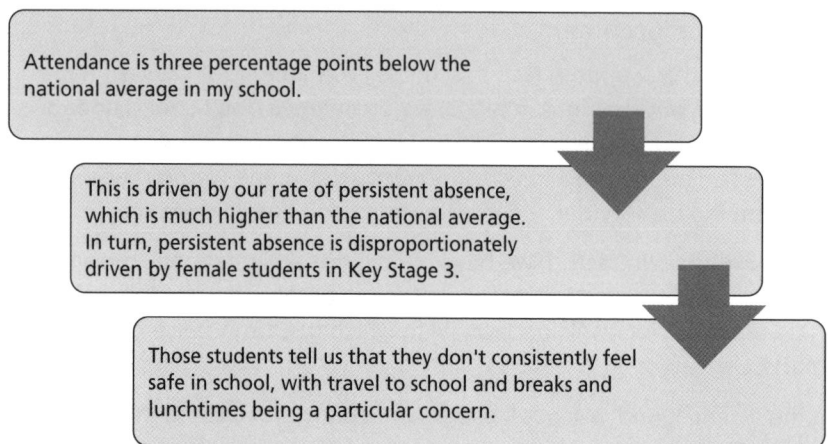

Figure 9.1: Three levels of depth – defining the challenge

Defining the change

Once you've spelled out the problem, you should have a much more precise sense of what changes might make a difference. For example, rather than reviewing generic attendance strategies, you can consider what you could do to help students to feel safer and supported as they take public transport to school.

This can then be elaborated into a theory of change. Often deployed in the third sector and research projects, theories of change are less widely used in school leadership. In essence, they describe the steps that connect the activities that you undertake towards the impact that you want to achieve, and what has to happen for that link to happen (Mayne, 2015; Reinholz and Andrews, 2020).

There are different forms of a theory of change, but a simple model can look like **Figure 9.2**:

Strategic evaluation for school leadership

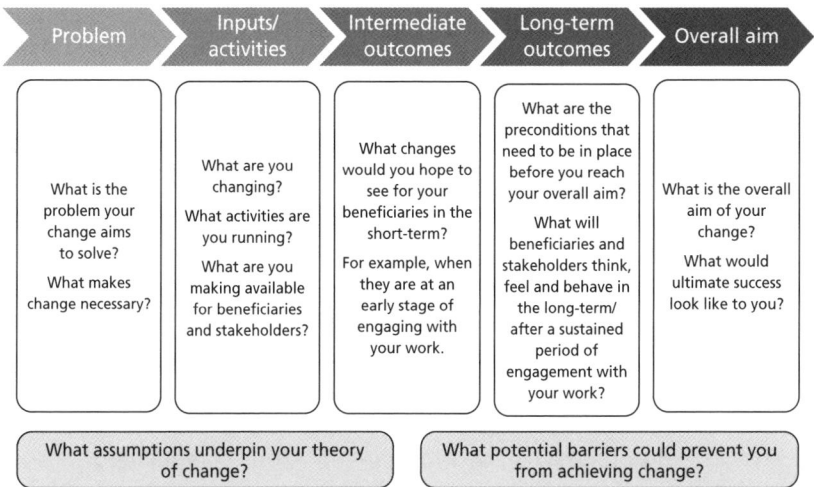

Figure 9.2: Example model of a theory of change

Populating a model like this helps you to:

- document the challenge that you have defined (e.g. rates of persistent absence in Key Stage 3)
- clearly set out the activities to address that challenge (e.g. improving student experience of travelling to school)
- outline the intermediate outcomes that you might expect to see in the shorter term (e.g. students feel safer or have fewer issues on a daily basis)
- indicate the long-term outcomes that might result (e.g. improved attendance)
- clarify the end goal of that change (e.g. improved student outcomes).

This process can help you to be clear and precise on the outcomes that will tell you whether you've been successful in your change, making effective evaluation much easier.

Defining success

Finally, you need to think about what to measure and why. It is important to approach this exercise from first principles. Rather than assuming that all interventions should be measured by improved student outcomes, it's crucial to ensure that what you are assessing aligns with your theory of change.

Measures that you might consider include:

- **administrative data:** the sorts of information that you are likely to collect anyway in a school environment, such as assessment, attendance or behaviour data
- **student or staff voice:** for example, using externally validated questionnaires of factors such as student motivation or staff wellbeing
- **observational data:** such as case studies or structured observations of lessons.

In the next section, we'll cover more detail on the data that you might use and how this process can be brought to life, but triangulating different data sources, thinking carefully about how you attribute impact (for example, trialling a change with one group but not another to compare the progress of the two) and being aware of the inherent limitations of any method that you use are likely to boost your chances of getting actionable data from evaluations.

Gathering and interpreting data

Most leaders will review data on a regular basis. Using this for high-quality evaluation means paying attention to:

- **Sample:** Who is the data from and at what scale? Can this be generalised across your school or trust or is this relevant only to a specific student group? Is the sample large enough to enable reliable insights to be drawn?
- **Collection methods:** What data are you collecting and how? Is it collected under standardised conditions? Are there factors to do with timing or location of data collection that could influence results?
- **Tools:** Are you using standardised or quality-assured assessments, or designing your own evaluation tools? Do the tools that you use come with benchmarks to compare against?
- **Frequency:** Do you have pre- and post-change measurements to track progress over time? Can you compare the data that you have to a group that is not participating in the intervention?

Looking at these factors together should help to protect against the biases and assumptions that can inevitably arise when interpreting data to inform decision-making.

This doesn't mean confining yourself to academic assessment only. Good-quality tools exist for measuring the development of skills beyond academic competencies – for example, Duckworth and Seligman (2005) used multiple measures of self-control with a group of Year 9 students, including student, teacher and parent questionnaires. Aggregating these measures together proved a significantly better predictor of end-of-year academic outcomes than IQ tests. Similarly, when it comes to measures such as student wellbeing, a range of high-quality tools exist – for example, the Warwick-Edinburgh Mental Wellbeing Scale (Clarke et al., 2011) and the Stirling Children's Well-being Scale (Liddle and Carter, 2015). Using these tools to assess outcomes beyond the academic, rather than in-house questionnaires, is likely to lead to more reliable insights.

Finally, the use of multiple indicators can be particularly powerful. If results from measures are all pointing the same way, this may help to provide greater confidence in the impact – or not – of any changes made. Examples of this kind of practice include:

- using multiple measures for different stakeholders (e.g. parents, teachers, children) and triangulating outcomes
- cross-referencing survey data with more objective administrative data; in education, this could be things like attainment, attendance or behaviour incidents
- using basic statistical tests to give us an idea of the uncertainty associated with any claim that we might make.

Bringing this together

School-based evaluation has significant limitations. Sample sizes can be limited, restricting the claims that you can make. Practically gathering the data that you need to make decisions is not without challenges. School environments are noisy, messy and not always easy environments for research-informed practice to develop.

At the same time, all evaluation has limits. Even large-scale randomised trials are not always as informative as we might like (Lortie-Forgues and Inglis, 2019). Often it is the combination of using the best external evidence from large trials with considered local implementation and evaluation that proves the magic combination.

Done well, strategic evaluation can empower leaders to focus on what is making the most difference to the students in their care. Even the simple process of planning with impact in mind can be transformative. Good evaluation should be a key part of the toolbox for any leader looking to make a radical difference in the lives of young people.

LEADERSHIP INSIGHT

Multi-layered evaluation

Angela Schofield, School Improvement and Oracy Advisor, UK

I don't think I'm alone among school leaders in having had more training and experience in monitoring than effective evaluation. There is a clear difference. Monitoring is about checking for fidelity, for compliance. Have we implemented what we were asked to implement, in the way set out in the plan? And have all tasks been completed in the timescale given? To what extent is this now embedded in classroom practice? Evaluation, on the other hand, is about objectively identifying the impact of that implementation. Has what we have done led to sustained positive impact on student outcomes? Which students benefited? What were the active ingredients that made the difference?

There are two elements of my evaluation process that I believe had a significant impact on the rigour of my evaluations, and therefore the validity of the conclusions used to inform decision-making. The first is that the intended impact of a strategy must be clearly established prior to implementation and communicated to those involved in delivery. The second element is dispassionate evaluation. We are all humans and have an innate desire to show that we have done the work and done it well. It's almost impossible to avoid the bias when evaluating the impact of our own work.

I wanted an evaluation process that incorporated stakeholder voice and data to reflect more than just academic outcomes. Guskey's five levels of evaluation (2016) is the model that I use to evaluate the impact of professional development (PD), which is a core element of all our implementation plans. Schools are VUCA environments (volatile, uncertain, complex and ambiguous) and Guskey's model is multi-layered, thus reflecting this.

- The first level is **participants' reactions** – do they feel that the plan is useful and relevant to their context? Was the training appropriate for their needs? While positive initial reactions don't guarantee success, they do indicate the level of buy-in.
- The second level is **participants' learning** – what new knowledge or understanding have they gained from the training? This allows me to check that the key messages and active ingredients have been communicated clearly.
- The third level is **organisational support and change** – we ask whether or not school leaders and staff feel that they have had sufficient support from the school and trust to implement the strategy. We also ask about changes to school processes and practices to support the new strategy.
- The fourth level is **participants' use of the new knowledge** – this is critical. While they might clearly articulate the new understanding, have they been willing and able to change their classroom practice as a result? This tells me whether additional PD or coaching is needed.
- Finally, we consider the impact on **student learning outcomes**. This includes all outcomes, and not just those that are academic. Even if all the responses to the previous levels were overwhelmingly positive, if the strategy hadn't had an impact on student outcomes, we would de-implement and begin at the explore phase again.

Developing my understanding of effective evaluation has transformed the way in which I implement projects. I can now track initial enthusiasm and understanding of the PD and ensure that this translates to changes in classroom practice, because I can spot gaps between initial understanding and teacher behaviour, putting individual coaching or group PD in place as needed. Guskey's model also considers the often-overlooked importance of changes at school and trust level. While teaching staff may be willing and knowledgeable enough to change their practice, without changes in systems, processes and resource allocation, the changes may not be long-term or, indeed, implemented in the first place. The ability to identify this as the implementation gap means that issues can be addressed. In several projects, understanding that this is the issue has made the difference between successful and misguided implementation. The fifth level – the impact on student outcomes – is critical. No matter how popular or well understood the changes, if they are not having the intended impact on outcomes, it is an inefficient use of limited resources with the associated opportunity cost.

Setting an intended impact measure before implementation and using Guskey's model have ensured that my evaluation is more nuanced, accurate and focused, meaning that projects are now more likely to lead to sustained improvements in practice and, therefore, student outcomes.

> ## Questions for reflection
> - Look at the last strategic plan you wrote or contributed to. How deeply was the challenge that the plan addressed defined? Did you go to the root causes – the problem behind the problem?
> - How consistent are you in defining the difference between intermediate and long-term outcomes? For long-term changes, such as improvements in attainment, have you defined the steps that will help you get there?
> - Do you always communicate to your colleagues that evaluation is not about demonstrating effectiveness and that it should instead be a tool to improve?

References

Clarke A, Friede T, Putz R et al. (2011) Warwick-Edinburgh Mental Wellbeing Scale (WEMWBS): Validated for teenage school students in England and Scotland. A mixed methods assessment. *BMC Public Health* 11: 487.

Duckworth AL and Seligman MEP (2005) Self-discipline outdoes IQ in predicting academic performance of adolescents. *Association for Psychological Science* 16(12): 939–944.

Durlak JA and DuPre EP (2008) Implementation matters: A review of research on the influence of implementation on program outcomes and the factors affecting implementation. *American Journal of Community Psychology* 41(3): 327–350.

Education Endowment Foundation (EEF) (2018) *Teaching and Learning Toolkit*. Available at: https://educationendowmentfoundation.org.uk/evidence-summaries/teaching-learning-toolkit/ (accessed 11 September 2024).

Education Endowment Foundation (EEF) (2023) *Annual reports*. Available at: https://educationendowmentfoundation.org.uk/about-us/annual-reports (accessed 27 September 2024).

Guskey TR (2016) Gauge impact with 5 levels of data. *Learning Forward* 37(1): 32–37.

ImpactEd (2024) *Report 2 – Understanding Attendance: Implementing strategies with impact*. Available at: https://www.impactedgroup.uk/research-campaigns-and-resources/understanding-attendance-report-2-e5bae (accessed 27 September 2024).

Kluger A and DeNisi A (1996) The effects of feedback interventions on performance: A historical review, a meta-analysis, and a preliminary feedback intervention theory. *Psychological Bulletin* 119(2): 254–284.

Liddle I and Carter GF (2015) Emotional and psychological well-being in children: The development and validation of the Stirling Children's Well-being Scale. *Educational Psychology in Practice* 31(2): 174–185.

Lortie-Forgues H and Inglis M (2019) Rigorous large-scale educational RCTs are often uninformative: Should we be concerned? *Educational Researcher* 48(3): 158–166.

Mayne J (2015) Useful theory of change models. *Canadian Journal of Program Evaluation* 30(2): 121.

Reinholz DL and Andrews TC (2020) Change theory and theory of change: What's the difference anyway? *International Journal of STEM Education* 7(2). DOI: 10.1186/s40594-020-0202-3.

SECTION 2 – PART 2
Professional practice: Leading a professional culture

PROFESSIONAL PRINCIPLE 7

Establish a culture of high expectations and a strong sense of belonging

CHAPTER 10: CASE STUDY

Creating an inclusive culture: Why culture matters at St Matthew's and the ethos that underpins our 'why'

Sonia Thompson, Headteacher, St Matthew's CE Primary School, UK

This chapter will consider:
- why school culture is important
- how to create a culture for student success, including high expectations, inclusion and belonging
- how to create a culture where staff can thrive, including collegiality, professional trust, support and challenge.

This chapter explores key aspects of the culture at my school, a Church of England primary school in Birmingham, where vision and mission align and are pivotal to our school's success. It introduces why it is important and, using research, what is needed to create a culture where students, teachers and school communities can flourish and thrive. The chapter emphasises the connections between having an inclusive culture and the principles and practices that support schools to enable, enact and maintain it.

Creating an inclusive culture: Why culture matters at St Matthew's and the ethos that underpins our 'why'

Setting a clear mission

Within education, culture is vociferously discussed and written about in many educational texts and, like all schools, we would like to think that we have a powerful culture. Although our values may be similar to those of other schools, our mission and mottos set the standard for what we want our culture to enable us to achieve.

> Mission statement: St Matthew's is a community of learners, planning, pursuing and providing excellence and enjoyment through Christian values. Children are valued for their individuality and heritage. They are supported and motivated to fulfil their potential, to meet the challenges of a changing society.
>
> Mottos: 'With God, nothing is impossible' and 'You are the light of the world'.

Much of our mission is bound to us being a church school. But over the years, as the school has lived and breathed, our culture has defined itself and cemented the story of our 'why'.

Our mission and mottos set the standard for our culture. They mean that our curriculum intent is clear. As Mary Myatt (2016, p. 38) states, 'we know what we are offering to our children and the reason why'. We built on this through our defining values – CAP – and now our culture has become an embodiment of high expectations and challenge for all.

> 'The St Matthew's Way' Values – **CAP**:
>
> - Team St Matthew's does not give up. We look back in history to prepare ourselves for the future – **courage**.
> - Team St Matthew's focuses on results and we do whatever it takes to achieve our goals. We push ourselves beyond what we think is possible – **attainment**.
> - Team St Matthew's values excellence in all that we do. We think and act as our own best selves – **pride**.

Our mottos, vision and values set the standard for our excellence. When we composed the mission statement, all members of our school community were involved and our brief was simple: to succinctly capture our ambition for our students and for each other. We wanted it to have longevity and to be able to hold us accountable. We wanted it to ensure that we always do our utmost for our students, in order for them to succeed.

Enacting and maintaining our mission and values

The 'St Matthew's Way' is a phrase that is often used about our school. It epitomises the high expectations, challenge and ambition that we have for our students and for each other. There is a sense of pride when visitors say that they can feel 'it' as soon as they walk through the door and are greeted warmly by a student. 'It' – our culture – is unique to our context because our school community has shaped it by deciding what we wanted for our school. So, if we wanted our students to greet visitors, we had to teach them to do that. If we wanted exceptional behaviour, we had to deliberately teach, model and then insist on and expect it every day – which is what we did!

We believe it is our culture that has enabled our students to live and breathe this ethos. Through high expectations around behaviour and building their attitudes to learning, our students want to learn and they love to learn. That is what they tell us. Their eagerness to learn and to challenge themselves is infectious and drives our determination to do whatever we can to realise this. It has led to students confidently being able to talk about what they have learned and remembered, and years of consistently strong outcomes.

Over the years, as our culture has embedded, it has enabled our teachers to become even more deliberate about driving forward a culture of excellence. This certainly needs to be deliberately driven. Allison and Tharby (2015) comment on the fact that excellence is hard to come by, and to achieve it, a child must work hard and be prepared to face the setbacks that they will inevitably meet. To support this, we talk about excellence as an everyday norm through our daily assemblies, but we are always mindful not just to talk about it but also to enact it, so that all students do well.

Andratesha Fritzgerald (2020, p. 11) writes: 'Sometimes we tout mission statements, vision statements, and goals that include buzzwords that everyone says and everyone can recite but only a few actually live the words out. You can tell what is most important by who is achieving the most.' This links to Coates (2017), who writes about the need to not only generate the appropriate culture but also that the concepts of mission, vision, values and culture must have synergy. It is this need to synergise that shaped the most recent reviews of our culture. It led us to think harder about equity and inclusion.

Building an equitable and inclusive curriculum and culture

We wanted an equitable and inclusive culture to act as the cornerstone for our high expectations around teaching, learning, behaviour and learning behaviours, for all students. This is particularly pertinent as most of our students are classed as disadvantaged and are from global majority backgrounds, as are many of our teachers. In thinking deeply about equity and inclusion, we are committed to the need for a co-existence between and deference to the rich cultural capital that our students and teachers bring to our school – what we call their 'existing capital'. Gonzalez et al. (2005) refer to this as 'funds of knowledge' and state that these are the 'rich repositories of accumulated knowledge found present in households and communities' (p. 9). Their work has supported us to make use of the space within our curriculum to not just acknowledge heritage and culture, but to place their deep richness at the heart of our curriculum.

Gonzalez et al. (2005, p. 15) write that 'understanding the funds of knowledge within a community and a family is important for a teacher. He/she can tap into this knowledge and use it to help acquire new knowledge.' At St Matthew's, we do this through the 'Ours' themes, which sit alongside our curriculum. Through these, we are able to share stories about our families and culture, including where our families are from and why they came to the UK. Our teachers have shared stories about their heritage and the things that they value. This can be seen at the beginning of each of our subject weeks. Students, families and teachers 'share their literacy lives' and benefit greatly from learning about each other and what makes us the diverse humans that we are. Our whole-school themes, called 'The Six Ours', enable this. We begin the year with 'Our Lives, Our Family' and go on to 'Our Community', 'Our World', 'Our Passions', 'Our Global Village' and finally, 'Our Future'.

Engaging with families

Our determination to engage with parents and families means that we also have an open-door policy, and a dedicated 'Parents to School Day' every half-term. Parents can then directly offer input into all foundation subject teaching. It also provides an opportunity for us to invite other agencies and people into our school who can support our parents' social and emotional needs. These include our local counsellor and Early Help. Cremin et al. (2004, p. 119) state, 'Many schools view parents primarily as supporters of schoolwork, rather than seeing them as a source of different and/or complementary literacy and learning experiences.' It is this reciprocity that has strengthened and widened our community. It has helped to grow and cement a sense of belonging, within and across our school community. This sits alongside an equitable and inclusive culture, where all are valued.

This wider vision for our students and for ourselves as educators has brought us so far but, like many other schools, we are never complacent. Like curriculum, our culture – mission, mottos and values – must be responsive and enable us, 'a community of learners', as our mission states, 'to plan, pursue and provide excellence and enjoyment'. For us, this next step was to become more evidence informed.

Creating an evidence-informed culture for staff

Our aim was to have a culture where staff thrived, through a focus on evidence-informed professional development, trust, support and challenge. We wanted our staff to feel that there was room within, between and across our non-negotiables for them to develop both professionally and socially. This included in-school time to ensure that their mental health and wellbeing were attended to. In giving the same status to this as we did to professional development, teachers knew that all their needs were respected. It was about creating a culture where mutual respect is acknowledged, which in turn creates a culture where staff want to remain and flourish in the classroom.

Flourishing in the classroom is most certainly crucial. The Institute for Effective Education (Abercrombie and Haslam, 2021, p. 14) writes, 'If nothing changes in the classroom, then nothing changes', and poses the question, 'How do teachers change, and hopefully improve, their practice, and what role does research evidence have in this?'

The solution for us was to become a 'research-sensitive school', as outlined in the Institute for Effective Education report (Abercrombie and Haslam, 2021). The report describes this type of school as one which has created a culture that allows teachers to focus on what matters: teaching and learning. This was our aim, and at St Matthew's we now have teachers who are reflective practitioners, and a sense of collegiality among staff. They are happy to read more, share knowledge and expertise, work both alone and collaboratively, and build strong relationships with each other, families, governors and our wider partners. It is a culture of professional trust and challenge in action.

Reflections

In conclusion, I refer to Genders and Barber (2021), who sum up why school culture is so important: 'Through pursuing excellence in teaching and working together for the common good, we will be enacting social justice for every community.' For me, social justice is our ultimate outcome. A culture wherein student and staff success matter means that we can and will redress the equity imbalance, which often blurs the lines when working in an area of high disadvantage.

Questions for reflection

- How do you define and promote your culture and how is your culture exemplified consistently to students, staff, parents and your wider school community?
- How do you ensure meaningful and reciprocal engagement with parents and the wider community, positioning them as partners in your educational mission of high expectations, inclusion and success for all?
- What structures are in place to support a culture of teacher wellbeing and professional growth, allowing them the opportunity to thrive?

References

Abercrombie N and Haslam J (2021) *The Open Door: How to be a Research-Sensitive School*. Institute for Effective Education. Available at: https://teachingschool.learnat.uk/attachments/download.asp?file=122&type=pdf (accessed 14 November 2024).

Allison S and Tharby A (2015) *Making Every Lesson Count*. Carmarthen: Crown House Publishing.

Coates M (2017) Coping with rapid change. In: Sage R (ed) *Paradoxes in Education*. Rotterdam: Sense Publishers, pp. 85–92.

Cremin T, Mottram M, Collins FM et al. (2004) *Researching Literacy Lives: Building Communities Between Home and School*. Abingdon: Routledge.

Fritzgerald A (2020) *Antiracism and Universal Design for Learning: Building Expressways to Success*. Lynnfield, MA: CAST Inc.

Genders N and Barber P (2021) *Leading a culture of teacher excellence – National Professional Qualification partnership*. The Church of England. Available at: https://churchofengland.org/media/stories-and-features/leading-culture-teacher-excellence-national-professional-qualification (accessed 14 November 2024).

Gonzalez N, Moll LC and Amanti C (eds) (2005) *Funds of Knowledge: Theorising Practices in Households, Communities and Classrooms*. Marwah, NJ: Lawrence Erlbaum Associates.

Myatt M (2016) *High Challenge, Low Threat: Finding the Balance*. Woodbridge: John Catt Educational.

PROFESSIONAL PRINCIPLE 8

Focus on developing teacher expertise and a culture of high-quality teaching

CHAPTER 11

Developing teacher expertise

Sarah Cottinghatt, *Head of Learning Design, IRIS Connect, UK*

> **This chapter will consider:**
> - how professional development (PD) might be approached in order to meet the needs of teachers at different career stages
> - useful mechanisms that can help in designing PD in a way that is likely to support the development of classroom practice
> - practical steps leaders can take to support teachers to engage meaningfully with PD.

The quality of teachers makes a difference to student outcomes, which can impact students' lives far beyond school (Jackson et al., 2014). It therefore makes sense to focus on the quality of teachers' PD (Fletcher-Wood and Zuccollo, 2020), not only for inexperienced teachers, but with the knowledge that experienced teachers can meaningfully develop too (Papay and Kraft, 2015).

Yet there are obstacles to high-quality PD. Issues with teacher retention have put pressure on schools to continually induct new staff. In addition, time is a constant barrier. While we cannot always find more of it, we can use evidence and experience to ensure that we make the best use of the time that we do have.

In this chapter, we will delve further into the evidence to consider some practical steps that you might take, as a leader, to embed a culture that is conducive to developing highly effective teaching. We will look at this through the lens of four mindset shifts that can help you to take action and plan strategically for high-quality PD.

Four mindset shifts

1. Teacher learning – learning is learning

Learning to teach is different in many ways from student learning. For one thing, teachers are trying to manage an environment with (in many settings) around 30 students, and to support them in achieving an invisible goal – learning. However, there are key ways in which we benefit from viewing teacher learning as similar to student learning.

Much as students can benefit from being taught a coherent curriculum, teachers will often require a tailored approach to their development, based on their individual needs and goals. This means abandoning one-off INSET sessions that jump from idea to idea and only focus on theory – for example, an 'inspire and forget' approach (Evidence Based Education, 2023) – and instead adopting a sustained approach to developing teachers' knowledge and practice. We know that connecting to prior knowledge, revisiting topics and contextualising ideas and practices all support long-term learning, no matter the age of the learner (Ausubel, 2000).

It is important to consider the expertise level of teachers in the same way that teachers adapt their approach depending on varying student expertise. Take coaching teachers, for example. More experienced teachers may benefit from more facilitative approaches, which draw on this experience and support them to tackle the more novel problems that they are experiencing, or to break strongly held habits to form more effective ones (Goodrich, 2024). Less experienced teachers may benefit from a more direct approach, where the coach shares their mental model more readily and breaks teaching techniques down into clear steps.

One issue that we have, though, is how to determine the level of teacher expertise in a particular domain. Experience is necessary but not sufficient when it comes to expertise (Berliner, 1987). We should avoid making assumptions that experience equals expertise, and instead use a variety of methods to determine what teachers know and can do (Coe et al., 2014). This can take the form of low-stakes observations, questions to assess understanding, student voice and looking at students' work and test scores. Triangulating evidence can support us to better understand the needs of our teachers so that we can determine how to build meaningfully from where teachers are in terms of their expertise.

2. Forms – mechanisms

When we think about teacher PD, we often think about the form that it takes, such as coaching, lesson study and whole-school sessions. Our second mindset shift is to see the form that PD takes as the packaging rather than the gift. Form matters less than the mechanisms that it employs (Sims et al., 2023). The Education Endowment Foundation (EEF) (2021) presents 14 mechanisms that appear to drive effective development, arranged into four purposes of PD and presented in a helpful table by the team at Ambition Institute (Pointer, 2022):

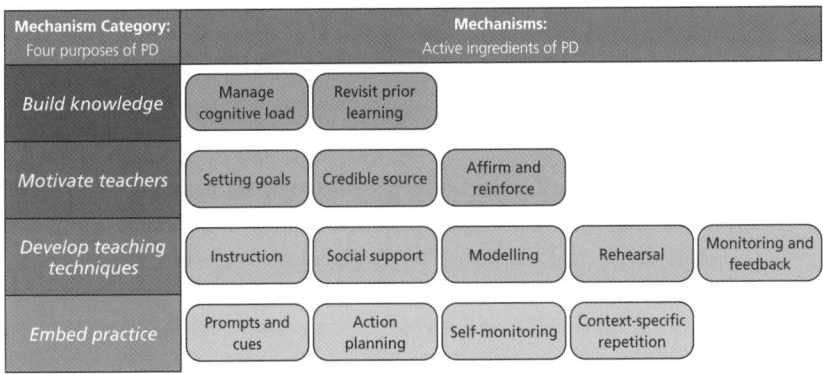

Table 10.1: 14 mechanisms that have a causal impact on student learning (Pointer, 2022, adapted from EEF, 2021). This figure has been reproduced with permission from Ambition Institute.

Mechanisms capture key ways in which forms of PD can best support teacher learning and behaviour change. When you adopt our first mindset shift (teacher learning to learning is learning), it becomes logical to focus on the mechanism of the PD driving learning, rather than simply the form itself. This is because the mechanisms drive learning rather than the form.

PD may be best designed and delivered with more mechanisms and with a balanced design (Sims et al., 2023), incorporating mechanisms from each of the four purposes – building knowledge, motivating staff, developing teaching techniques and embedding practice – since each of these is necessary for behaviour change (Sims et al., 2023). We can design and implement PD that harnesses these mechanisms, no matter the form of PD a school uses. Moving to a new form of PD takes time that could be better spent on other endeavours. Refining the school's ethos and approach instead, by baking in high-quality enactment of mechanisms, may be a better method. It is also particularly challenging to evaluate the impact of PD on student achievement. The mechanisms are a way in which to tentatively check and incrementally improve effectiveness. For example, a school that is using professional learning communities (PLCs) (where teachers work in groups to analyse practice) can use the mechanisms as one lens through which to evaluate the effectiveness of PLCs. We note that teachers are not necessarily changing their practice after the PLC discussion, and we can include the mechanisms of 'rehearsal' and 'action planning' to support teachers with this. This 'refine not replace' (Pointer, 2022) approach is likely to be time- and cost-effective compared with training staff to use another form of PD.

Of course, it is not what you do but the way that you do it (Major, 2017). When considering incorporating additional mechanisms into the school's PD, such as 'rehearsal', we should be clear on what it is and what it takes to use it well in our context. This is being both evidence informed and context driven. It may be a challenging culture shift to incorporate rehearsal into a school's PD, and the school may not see the positive results that they hope for. Careful implementation of mechanisms is necessary, which means considering the readiness of staff and systems in your context. For example, it may be quite a shift for a school to incorporate the mechanism 'manage cognitive load' into their PD if their current plans are to train teachers on many areas across the academic year. This may involve de-implementation to scale back and repurpose PD time. But more so, it will take buy-in from leaders who will need to understand that improvement is more likely if they focus on fewer changes and protect their staff from overload.

3. Control – alignment

How do we raise the bar for teaching in schools? We could take control by mandating the use of certain teaching techniques in particular ways and at particular times. But while mandating procedures may improve some teachers' practice, it runs the risk of limiting the effectiveness of others (Klein, 2011). This is because such an approach fails to acknowledge the complexity of teaching and the need for teachers to exercise judgement if they are to be more than technicians (Kavanagh et al., 2020).

We can instead think about creating alignment: movement towards the same goal but not necessarily doing the same things in the same way. The 'golden thread' that runs through teacher development programmes in England (DfE, 2022) is a large-scale example of an attempt to create alignment. From initial teacher training to executive headship, frameworks and the training programmes based on these draw on common evidence. This is a change that we can harness in schools. When staff have a similar understanding and shared language around teaching and learning, conversations are expedited and PD can be more effective. For example, coaching conversations are much richer if coach and coachee can examine a problem of practice in relation to a shared understanding of how people learn. A common language around codified teaching techniques can expedite the conversation so that we can weigh up which might be more appropriate to address the problem. More time can be spent developing teachers' judgement and practice. In addition, we can create alignment through the creation of symbiotic streams of PD: whole school, team and individual teacher. Sherrington (2021) explains how whole-school PD can support alignment around key evidence-informed frameworks and ideas; time in teams can be used to translate these ideas into subjects and phases (with support such as a meeting structure); and individual PD recognises that teachers have individual goals and motivations that require support and development.

When teachers have an aligned understanding of learning and what this might mean for teaching, we can, with confidence, support teachers to test and refine techniques without feeling that we must mandate how they are used. It is important to their success that teachers are given this opportunity to experiment with how techniques are implemented.

A review by Jørgensen et al. (2024) on the use of cognitive science approaches by 13 UK teachers observed the need for them to be able to experiment with approaches.

4. Routine expertise – adaptive expertise

Teachers operate in complex environments characterised by change and uncertainty (Davis and Sumara, 2007). This requires adaptive expertise. While routine expertise involves doing things in the same way each time, adaptive expertise involves the same benefits of efficiency as routine expertise (doing what works most of the time) plus being sensitive to cues that suggest the need for flex and to exercise judgement (Kavanagh et al., 2020). For example, a teacher does their entry routine the same way each lesson but is sensitive to a student who enters looking low and finds time to check in with them. If we mandate teaching techniques and expect to see them in teachers' lessons at particular times, then we are incentivising routine expertise and not the development of decision-making that is necessary for adaptive expertise.

To develop adaptive expertise, teachers may benefit from PD that causes them to think about why and when practices might be useful. This means that adaptive expertise is more than just behavioural changes in response to cues; it requires metacognition (Hu, 2024) – teachers must understand and augment their decision-making. Mechanisms of effective PD such as 'modelling' and 'rehearsal' can be used to develop teachers' adaptive expertise by breaking down teacher practices and recomposing them in meaningful ways, rather than teaching them one way in which to enact a technique (Banks et al., 2024). This encourages metacognitive talk around the purpose and context of effective use of the technique. Because teaching is constantly changing (new classes, curriculum developments, etc.), even experienced teachers benefit from PD that helps them to tackle the novel problems that they are experiencing.

Adaptive expertise is about teachers having efficient habits and being flexible. However, habits can make it difficult for teachers, particularly experienced teachers, to improve (Feldon, 2007). This means that when planning their PD, we should incorporate mechanisms that help teachers to change habits, such as supporting them to practise new techniques in context (Hobbiss et al., 2021).

Next steps

Making effective choices about how to spend limited PD time is tough and has led to approaches that we would never consider as great learning opportunities if they were delivered to students. The mindset shifts in this chapter, if adopted, become better lenses through which we can design and deliver PD. These involve, to a large extent, treating teacher learning similarly to student learning, and ensuring that teacher PD is designed, delivered and evaluated with mechanisms in mind. However, we also need to think about the environment in which teachers operate. Teachers need to be adaptive to meet the changing needs of students. PD that develops teachers' judgement can better equip them for the changes the role may bring throughout their careers.

> ## Questions for reflection
> - Do staff share a common understanding of learning and the implications for teaching? How did you build this? How might you better achieve this?
> - How well does your current PD harness mechanisms?
> - How does your PD support teachers to change habits, embed approaches and build adaptive expertise?
> - What is the culture around PD in your setting? How do you show staff that their development is valued? Do staff feel supported and empowered to try out new ideas and push themselves beyond their comfort zones?

References

Ausubel DP (2000) *The Acquisition and Retention of Knowledge: A Cognitive View.* Dordrecht: Springer Science and Business Media.

Banks B, Sims S, Curran J et al. (2024) *Decomposition and recomposition: Effects on novice teachers' enactment and transfer of behaviour management practices.* Ambition Institute. Available at: https://s3.eu-west-2.amazonaws.com/ambition-institute/documents/Decomp-Recomp_2024_Full_paper_digital.pdf (accessed 5 November 2024).

Berliner DC (1987) Ways of thinking about students and classrooms by more and less experienced teachers. In: Calderhead J (ed) *Exploring Teachers' Thinking.* London: Cassell Education, pp. 60–83.

Coe R, Aloisi C, Higgins S et al. (2014) *What makes great teaching? Review of the underpinning research.* The Sutton Trust. Available at: https://suttontrust.com/wp-content/uploads/2014/10/What-Makes-Great-Teaching-REPORT.pdf (accessed 5 November 2024).

Davis B and Sumara D (2007) Complexity science and education: Reconceptualizing the teacher's role in learning. *Interchange* 38: 53–67.

Department for Education (DfE) (2022) *Delivering world-class professional development.* Available at: https://assets.publishing.service.gov.uk/media/62850bddd3bf7f1f433ae149/Delivering_world_class_teacher_development_policy_paper.pdf (accessed 23 September 2024).

Education Endowment Foundation (EEF) (2021) *Effective Professional Development: Guidance Report.* Available at: https://educationendowmentfoundation.org.uk/education-evidence/guidance-reports/effective-professional-development (accessed 11 December 2024).

Evidence Based Education (2023) *Our Theory of Change.* Available at: https://evidencebased.education/our-theory-of-change/ (accessed 18 December 2024).

Feldon DF (2007) Cognitive load and classroom teaching: The double-edged sword of automaticity. *Educational Psychologist* 42(3): 123–137.

Fletcher-Wood H and Zuccollo J (2020) *The effects of high-quality professional development on teachers and students: A rapid review and meta-analysis.* Education Policy Institute. Available at: https://epi.org.uk/wp-content/uploads/2020/02/EPI-Wellcome_CPD-Review__2020.pdf (accessed 5 November 2024).

Goodrich J (2024) *Responsive Coaching: Evidence-Informed Instructional Coaching That Works for Every Teacher in Your School.* Woodbridge: John Catt Educational.

Hobbiss M, Sims S and Allen R (2021) Habit formation limits growth in teacher effectiveness: A review of converging evidence from neuroscience and social science. *Review of Education* 9(1): 3–23.

Hu Y (2024) *Reconceptualizing Teacher Adaptability: The Teacher Adaptive-Cognition Theory.* PhD thesis, Michigan State University. Available at: https://d.lib.msu.edu/etd/51728 (accessed 18 December 2024).

Jackson CK, Rockoff JE and Staiger DO (2014) Teacher effects and teacher-related policies. *Annual Review of Economics* 6(1): 801–825.

Jørgensen CR, Perry T and Lea R (2024) The enactment of cognitive science informed approaches in the classroom – teacher experiences and contextual dimensions. *British Journal of Educational Studies* 72(1): 43–62.

Kavanagh SS, Metz M, Hauser M et al. (2020) Practicing responsiveness: Using approximations of teaching to develop teachers' responsiveness to students' ideas. *Journal of Teacher Education* 71(1): 94–107.

Klein GA (2011) *Streetlights and Shadows: Searching for the Keys to Adaptive Decision Making.* Cambridge, MA: The MIT Press.

Major LE (2017) Is the Bananarama principle dead? In: *The Sutton Trust News & Opinion*. Available at: https://suttontrust.com/news-opinion/all-news-opinion/is-the-bananarama-principle-dead (accessed 23 September 2024).

Papay JP and Kraft MA (2015) Productivity returns to experience in the teacher labor market: Methodological challenges and new evidence on long-term career improvement. *Journal of Public Economics* 130: 105–119.

Pointer N (2022) Refine not replace: A 'mechanism-first' approach to teacher education. In: *Ambition Institute blog*. Available at: https://ambition.org.uk/blog/refine-not-replace-a-mechanism-first-approach-to-teacher-education (accessed 23 September 2024).

Sherrington T (2021) Planning professional learning: One system; three streams. In: *teacherhead.com*. Available at: https://teacherhead.com/2021/02/21/planning-professional-learning-one-system-three-streams (accessed 5 November 2024).

Sims S, Fletcher-Wood H, O'Mara-Eves A et al. (2023) *Effective teacher professional development: New theory and a meta-analytic test*. Centre for Education Policy and Equalising Opportunities, University College London. Available at: chrome-extension://efaidnbmnnnibpcajpcglclefindmkaj/https://repec-cepeo.ucl.ac.uk/cepeow/cepeowp22-02.pdf (accessed 5 November 2024).

PROFESSIONAL PRINCIPLE 9

Establish effective systems and processes that support teaching and learning

CHAPTER 12

Taking it forward: Supporting systems

Katy Chedzey, Associate Director, Professional Learning and Accreditation, Chartered College of Teaching, UK

The professional principles discussed throughout this book have sought to provide insight into some of the practices that evidence suggests might contribute to effective school leadership, and which therefore might be of value for school leaders to implement in their settings. It is likely that you will already be doing good work in many of these areas, yet you may also have identified some opportunities to strengthen existing practice in light of your reading.

In terms of taking this work forward, it's vital to consider some of the structural and operational factors that might influence successful implementation. The Education Endowment Foundation's (EEF) (2024) guide to implementation for schools provides a useful reminder of why this is important:

> It is all too easy to 'dream big' when thinking about implementing a new programme or practice and overlook the structural conditions that make it possible. While implementation is fundamentally a social process, it relies on a range of systems and structures that create the conditions for those interactions to occur ... Systems and structures are important because they allow people to enact the behaviours that drive effective implementation. (p. 16)

Efficient and effective systems and structures are integral to the smooth running of a school and there is a consensus in the evidence base around school leadership that the most effective school leaders are skilled in managing personnel and resources, optimising how these are used to support teaching and learning (Grissom et al., 2021), ensuring the physical school environment is conducive to learning (Day and Sammons, 2020), and establishing a safe and orderly environment, which includes establishing clear and consistent approaches to behaviour (Robinson et al., 2009).

Ineffective systems and processes can significantly hinder our ability to make progress. For example, we can all understand that in a school where behaviour is not managed effectively, it's unlikely that we'd see the culture of high expectations described by Sonia Thompson in the preceding chapter. Instead, an ineffective behaviour system would make it more likely that teachers experience high levels of disruption, thus taking their time away from teaching and learning, ultimately impacting on student outcomes. Surveys of teachers consistently tell us that behaviour is one of the most significant challenges they face in their classrooms, and this issue is getting worse (Teacher Tapp, 2024). So, for school leaders, the focus must be on how we might help to address such problems. Behaviour can be considered to be one of the 'wicked problems' that were mentioned in Sarah Cottinghatt's chapter on developing teacher expertise – it's a complex issue where there is no one clear solution. This means that schools will, of course, need to adapt their approach to respond to the needs of their specific context. However, the need to have systems and structures to support this approach is universal.

LEADERSHIP INSIGHT

Evaluating a school behaviour system

Sam Vickers, CEO, Batley Multi Academy Trust, UK

When undertaking the Chartered Status pathway, Sam Vickers identified an opportunity to inquire around their school behaviour system as part of the school practice inquiry project assessment. Here, Sam describes their approach and reflects on what they learnt from the process.

In my previous role as the headteacher of a school within our trust, staff had worked incredibly hard to raise standards in every area. The quality of teaching had improved significantly, the curriculum was redesigned to meet the requirements of the national curriculum and adapted to suit the community needs and requirements, and careers permeated all aspects of the school's work. The next phase of the school-improvement journey was the further development of the behaviour-for-learning strategy to maximise progress. Implementing a new behaviour policy had been a key element of the initial improvement journey, but the original policy no longer met the school's needs as we shifted away from a need to eradicate higher-tariff behaviours, and moved towards reducing low-level disruption and developing more intrinsic motivation. The aim was to no longer settle for mediocrity where good is 'good enough', but rather for students to be the best version of themselves in all aspects of their work and in their social and personal interactions.

In looking for solutions, I undertook a detailed, evidence-informed inquiry to evaluate current effectiveness of our behaviour approach, engaging staff within that process to adapt, refine, embed and sustain key aspects of effective practice around behaviour.

A variety of different methods of collecting qualitative and quantitative data were utilised, including paper-based questionnaires, digital surveys, one-to-one interviews, and lesson observations across Years 7 to 11 and across a range of subject areas. The findings were interesting. Data analysis identified inconsistency as a major contributory factor in boys' underachievement, and that greater consistency in the application of school systems would benefit classroom practice overall, resulting in boys being more on task, with fewer incidences of low-level disruption. Teachers and associate staff felt that the system itself needed some adjustments, however, all those involved concurred that the consistent application of the system was the most crucial aspect of this work and pointed us towards some clear and specific areas of the policy where we could focus our attention.

From this initial inquiry I reflected on three key implications to take forward in my own leadership – the three Cs: clarity, communication and consistency.

Key aspects for clarity involve setting out the school's vision and values, being clear about what the policies are and why it is crucial staff and students adhere to these policies, and applying them consistently, fairly and equitably in all aspects of school life. This application of consistency helps to reduce teacher/staff workload, and ensures colleagues are able to collaborate effectively together. It also ensures a fair and equitable system for all. Staff time is one of the greatest resources available in schools and we must use it wisely, effectively and efficiently to maximise outcomes for all.

> The consistent application of evidence-informed policies and procedures is one of the most valuable tools we can use as leaders and can contribute to building school culture, as we are reminded in this quote from Schein (2004, p. 1):
>
> *Culture is both a dynamic phenomenon that surrounds us at all times, being constantly enacted and created by our interactions with others and shaped by leadership behaviour, and a set of structures, routines, rules and norms that guide and constrain behaviour.'*
>
> We must set our students – and teachers – up to succeed, and not simply assume that just because a policy has been written, it will be enacted as we had intended. Staff professional development and regular opportunity for two-way feedback between staff and senior leaders is a core part of this work. Similarly, by adopting the cycle of 'Plan, Do, Review and Evaluate' as a systematic part of an iterative cycle, we can better understand the effectiveness of the systems and processes we implement and be better positioned to achieve the long-term goals we are aiming towards.

Of course, behaviour systems are just one example from the many organisational systems and structures that enable teaching and learning to take place successfully.

Further areas that can be helpful to reflect on include, but are not limited to:

- **Staff resourcing:** How do you recruit, train and allocate staff to classes and activities in the most efficient and effective way?
- **Timetabling:** How do you maximise the time for learning across the curriculum, including minimising disruptions to the timetable wherever possible?
- **Facilitating teacher development:** How do you identify needs? How do you organise and resource teacher professional development, and how is this time protected?
- **Physical environment and resources:** Is the space in the school conducive to learning? Do teachers and students have access to the resources they need to enable the curriculum to be delivered as intended?
- **Workload and wellbeing:** How can you minimise unnecessary bureaucracy and workload that takes teachers away from attending

to teaching and learning? Where particular tasks are required, are there more efficient ways of teachers completing these? When implementing any system or policy, are you aware of any unintended consequences in terms of teacher workload and/or wellbeing?

The notion of 'unintended consequences' is useful to keep in mind not only when implementing new approaches, but also as part of any ongoing monitoring and review of school practices. Leaders who undertake Chartered Status with the Chartered College of Teaching complete a rigorous inquiry into an aspect of policy or practice, similar to that described by Sam Vickers above. Examining the wider impacts – intended or unintended – of any change to school practice is a core requirement of the process, with three key areas to consider.

The first of these is teacher workload. An awareness of the impacts of any policy or practice on teacher workload is an integral part of school development. Of course, there may indeed be times when school development activity leads to increased workload – even if that increase is just short term. Nonetheless, leaders have a responsibility to scrutinise systems and processes to understand the ways in which they may make demands on teachers' time, and take action where required to minimise unnecessary demands as much as possible. When leaders *do* require a significant time commitment from staff, they must be confident that the benefits outweigh the disadvantages, and could perhaps look to gain the time back by lessening the demands in other areas.

A second consideration relates to the budget and resource requirements associated with a system, policy or approach. For example, there may be initial training and resource costs, but what will the budget and resource demands be over the next one, three or five years in order to sustain this work, and how will this be incorporated into plans moving forward?

The final and perhaps most important area for leaders to consider relates to equalities and inclusion. As you will be aware, in line with the Equality Act (2010), all schools have an obligation to ensure that they do not discriminate against any individual with a protected characteristic.

When making changes to policy or practice, you must ensure that the change does not disadvantage or discriminate against anyone because of:

- sex
- race
- disability
- religion or belief
- sexual orientation
- gender reassignment
- pregnancy or maternity.

This applies not only to students. It is equally important to assess the impact of practices or policies on equalities for staff and others within the school community. Routinely undertaking an equality impact assessment as part of any policy- or systems-development work can help leaders to understand and mitigate any such impacts.

This is particularly important for leaders' work around equity and inclusion and should perhaps extend into all of the work you undertake as a leader. Grissom et al. (2021) consider the evidence around school leadership and argue that to make the greatest difference to outcomes for the most disadvantaged and marginalised students in schools, leaders need to adopt an equity lens throughout their work:

> We propose that the adoption of an equity lens inspires school leaders to reconsider their leadership behaviors in light of equity considerations, asking questions such as how their actions will remove barriers and create opportunities for historically underserved groups, how their behaviors will promote access to critical resources and supports for the success of all students, and how their practices will confront institutional factors that may be currently inhibiting certain members of the school community from achieving their full potential. Regular, authentic examination of these refracted leadership behaviors presents an opportunity for school leaders to advance equity and promote an antiracist school community.
> (Grissom et al., 2021, p. 74)

Final reflections: Embracing evidence-informed leadership

The fourteen professional principles discussed through the chapters of this book aim to provide an indication of what effective and evidence-informed school leadership *might* look like. The enactment of these principles will vary according to your role, context and where you are in your professional journey.

Professional knowledge

- Demonstrates comprehensive knowledge of teaching and learning, curriculum and assessment
- Has a deep understanding of their school(s), and also the wider educational context
- Understands the characteristics of effective professional development

Professional practice: Leading school development

- Has a clear vision, focused on achieving ambitious outcomes for all learners
- Takes an evidence-informed approach to school development
- Engages in critical evaluation and reflection to inform strategic choices

Professional practice: Leading a professional culture

- Focuses on developing teacher expertise and a culture of high-quality teaching
- Establishes a culture of high expectations and a strong sense of belonging
- Establishes effective systems and processes that support teaching and learning

Professional behaviours

| Critically evaluates and reflects on their own practice | Is committed to engaging in relevant, career-long professional learning | Exhibits and encourages collegiality by supporting, and learning from, others |

| Models high standards of professionalism | Engages critically with research and evidence |

In terms of *your* leadership journey, you are encouraged to reflect on these professional principles and utilise them to guide your own professional development. It's not uncommon for leaders to prioritise teacher professional development but somewhat neglect their own, so take some time to **reflect** on each principle, **consider any implications** for your own leadership development and practice, and perhaps **identify at least one action** that could help to progress what is likely to be an ongoing endeavour to embed evidence-informed leadership in your context.

A more detailed evaluation framework, including sub-principles for each of the professional principles discussed in this book, is published in the Chartered College of Teaching's 'Professional framework', which is available to access on our website.

References

Day C and Sammons P (2020) *Successful School Leadership.* Education Development Trust. Available at: https://edt.org/research-and-insights/successful-school-leadership-2020-publication/ (accessed 29 November 2024).

Education Endowment Foundation (EEF) (2024) *A School's Guide to Implementation: Guidance Report.* Available at: https://educationendowmentfoundation.org.uk/education-evidence/guidance-reports/implementation (accessed 15 December 2024).

Grissom J, Egalite A and Lindsay C (2021) *How Principals Affect Students and Schools: A Systematic Synthesis of Two Decades of Research.* New York: The Wallace Foundation. Available at: https://wallacefoundation.org/principalsynthesis (accessed 15 December 2024).

Robinson V, Hohepa M and Lloyd C (2009) *School Leadership and Student Outcomes: Identifying What Works and Why. Iterative Best Evidence Synthesis Programme.* Ministry of Education/University of Auckland. Available at: https://educationcounts.govt.nz/__data/assets/pdf_file/0015/60180/BES-Leadership-Web-updated-foreword-2015.pdf (accessed 15 December 2024).

Schein EH (2004) *Organisational Culture and Leadership*, 3rd ed. San Francisco, CA: Jossey-Bass.

Teacher Tapp (2024). Behaviour, Ofsted and fining parents. *Teachertapp*, 12 March. Available at: https://teachertapp.com/uk/articles/behaviour-ofsted-and-fining-parents/ (accessed 15 December 2024).

APPENDIX

Framework for ethical leadership in education

Ethical educational leadership is based on the 'Seven principles for public life':

1. **Selflessness**: Leaders should act solely in the interest of children and young people.
2. **Integrity**: Leaders must avoid placing themselves under any obligation to people or organisations that might try inappropriately to influence them in their work. Before acting and taking decisions, they must declare and resolve openly any perceived conflict of interest and relationships.
3. **Objectivity**: Leaders must act and take decisions impartially and fairly, using the best evidence and without discrimination or bias. Leaders should be dispassionate, exercising judgement and analysis for the good of children and young people.
4. **Accountability**: Leaders are accountable to the public for their decisions and actions and must submit themselves to the scrutiny necessary to ensure this.
5. **Openness**: Leaders should expect to act and take decisions in an open and transparent manner. Information should not be withheld from scrutiny unless there are clear and lawful reasons for so doing.
6. **Honesty**: Leaders should be truthful.
7. **Leadership**: Leaders should exhibit these principles in their own behaviour. They should actively promote and robustly support the principles and be willing to challenge poor behaviour wherever it occurs. Leaders include both those who are paid to lead schools and colleges and those who volunteer to govern them.

Schools and colleges serve children and young people and help them grow into fulfilled and valued citizens. As role models for the young, how we behave as leaders is as important as what we do. Leaders should show leadership through the following personal characteristics or virtues:

a. **Trust**: Leaders are trustworthy and reliable. We hold trust on behalf of children and should be beyond reproach. We are honest about our motivations.

b. **Wisdom**: Leaders use experience, knowledge and insight. We demonstrate moderation and self-awareness. We act calmly and rationally. We serve our schools and colleges with propriety and good sense.

c. **Kindness**: Leaders demonstrate respect, generosity of spirit, understanding and good temper. We give difficult messages humanely where conflict is unavoidable.

d. **Justice**: Leaders are fair and work for the good of all children. We seek to enable all young people to lead useful, happy and fulfilling lives.

e. **Service**: Leaders are conscientious and dutiful. We demonstrate humility and self-control, supporting the structures, conventions and rules which safeguard quality. Our actions protect high-quality education.

f. **Courage**: Leaders work courageously in the best interests of children and young people. We protect their safety and their right to a broad, effective and creative education. We hold one another to account courageously.

g. **Optimism**: Leaders are positive and encouraging. Despite difficulties and pressures, we are developing excellent education to change the world for the better.

The framework above has been adapted from ASCL (2019) *Navigating the educational moral maze: Final report of the Ethical Leadership Commission*. Available at: www.ascl.org.uk/ASCL/media/ASCL/Our%20view/Campaigns/Navigating-the-educational-moral-maze.pdf (accessed 27 March 2025).